GOD,
I
Know
You're
Here
Somewhere

Elizabeth Cody Newenhuyse

GOD, I Know You're Here Somewhere

BETHANY HOUSE PUBLISHERS
MINNEAPOLIS, MINNESOTA 55438

Published by Bethany House Publishers
A Ministry of Bethany Fellowship, Inc.
11300 Hampshire Avenue South
Minneapolis, Minnesota 55438

Printed in the United States of America.

Library of Congress Cataloging-in-Publication Data

Newenhuyse, Elizabeth Cody.

    God I know you're here somewhere : finding God in the clutter of life / Elizabeth Cody Newenhuyse.

      p. cm.

    ISBN 1–55661–512–4

    1. Women—Religious life. 2. Christian life.

3. Newenhuyse, Elizabeth Cody. I. Title.

BV4527N456   1996

248.8'43—dc20

                                     96–4444

                                       CIP

To the Family
at
Faith Covenant Church

ELIZABETH CODY NEWENHUYSE is the award-winning author of several books, including *Sometimes I Feel Like Running Away From Home* and *Am I the Only Crazy Mom on This Planet?*. She is also a retreat and conference speaker and a frequent contributor to *Today's Christian Woman* magazine. She lives with her husband, Fritz, and daughter, Amanda, near Chicago.

Contents

Introduction:
Will God Still Love Me
If I Don't Floss?

IS THIS YOU?

It's late evening. You're plodding around the house, picking up shoes and toys, getting lunches ready for the next day, straightening the kitchen. You wash up, not bothering to moisturize or floss. You consider laying out your clothes for the morning, decide against it, resign yourself to a rush. You would like to spend some time reading your Bible in bed, but you're just too tired.

As you get ready for bed, half listening to the odd whistling sound your husband is making as he sleeps, you feel guilty. Ruth Graham would take the time to read God's Word. (And Billy would be propped up on his side of the bed, glasses perched on his nose, reading *his* Bible. Bet you anything *he* wouldn't be sprawled out snoring.) Or Mother Teresa. She would be on her tiny knees in nighttime prayer. None of this cursory "thank-you-God-for-my-family" stuff for her. You recall reading how Catherine Marshall suffered from insomnia and used her wakeful times to commune with the Almighty, praying and reading and writing. When you can't sleep, you go eat a dish of ice cream. (Well, it *is* milk, and milk is a sedative.)

You jerk the covers over from your husband's side—he has a way of hogging them, leaving you half-exposed and freezing—and think again about Mother Teresa, off in India helping those who have no covers, doing great things for God. *What have you done for God lately?* Then your mind drifts westward, to California, where Joni Eareckson Tada lives. She can't even get into bed without assistance, but does she complain? No, she uses her disability to draw closer to her Creator. Bedridden Amy Carmichael . . . blind Fanny Crosby . . . frail Theresa of Avila. Your friend from college who now ministers among the inner-city poor.

And then there's you.

How does God use you? you wonder. In a mighty or minuscule way? Is God even with you most of the time?

You drop off to sleep, wondering . . . wondering . . .

. . . and then you get up the next day and rush off and it begins all over again.

You've sat and listened to pastors and speakers say nice, upbeat words about how God loves you, God never leaves you, God can use you . . . yes, you! You leave the service or the seminar feeling energized and uplifted, ready to take on the world, confident that you are walking—no, striding—with the Lord.

And then Monday comes, and it's raining, and slowly the rosy glow fades away as real life sets in.

I've been that speaker, encouraging women in their Christian walk. I've looked out from a lectern at their faces and wondered what awaited them at home. I've wondered what awaited *me* at home. Is God there, too?

The correct, approved spiritual response is, "Of course He's there. God is always with you." We believe that, but do we *feel* it? Have you ever secretly wondered, *Is God with me as I*

- force my dog to gag down a heartworm pill?
- stand in drizzle and mud, pretending to enjoy yet another soccer game?

- sit in my windowless office cubicle, neck and back aching, staring at numbers on a screen?
- cut my hand on a can as I separate the recyclables?
- argue with my husband (about the same thing, yet again)?

Where is God when I stand at the sink slamming pots and pans around in a hormonal sulk, when I hear that friends at church are building an expensive new house and I have to choke back envy because *we* can't even afford matching dining room chairs? Maybe He's with me, but does He like being with me? Am I good company for God? Sometimes *I* don't like being with me, but I'm sort of stuck.

Is He there in the mundane as well as the magnificent, with trivial me as well as with Mother Teresa and Theresa of Avila and Esther and Elizabeth and Ruth and Mary? What have I done with my life up till now?

Dear God, is this all there is? Am I all I can be? And how can I see your face, feel the touch of your hand?

God, how can I get through to you in the midst of . . . well, in the midst of real life? I don't think you have a beeper number as you go about doing mighty works. I don't feel very mighty, Lord. I'm just me. I make mistakes. I procrastinate. I don't make the most of my gifts. I'm way behind in the "daily" devotional reading.

Father, will you still love me if I don't always floss or feed my houseplants or follow up on a promise? I don't know a lot, but I do know I love you in my own stumbling way. I love you, and I'm listening . . . .

1
And Suddenly God . . .

YOU'RE PROBABLY FAMILIAR WITH the story of St. Augustine's conversion, how he heard the voice of Christ and ran out into his garden, where he fell to his knees and surrendered his life to the Lord. Saints like Augustine who lived hundreds of years ago and people in inspirational articles and books are always having these direct encounters with the Divine. You know, "I hated my life and we went broke and the dog died and we lost everything in a killer hailstorm and I asked God, 'Why?' and one day I was walking along and suddenly God . . ."

- Suddenly God helped her realize what her problem was.
- Suddenly God was there with His reassuring presence.
- Suddenly God prompted them as to what their course should be.

It all sounds so neat. And maybe it is if you're an Augustine-type saint. Trouble is, most of us aren't, and most of us don't have some gripping story of divine intervention to share with others. (Do you personally know anyone who prayed for money and the *exact amount* came in the mail from an anonymous source?)

I don't mean to sound cynical or dismissive. There have been a few "suddenly Gods" in my life, those no-doubt-about-it incidents when I've been flooded with awareness of His indwelling presence. I became a Christian that way. No, God didn't speak to me in Latin as He apparently did to Augustine. I didn't hear anything. But as a searching and sometimes rebellious twenty-something, I *felt* the living Christ in a wraparound sort of love that I can only liken to a parent who gently, but firmly, grabs hold of a thrashing and disobedient child and says, "Stop. It's all right. I'm here."

Since then I have experienced several other occasions when my life felt directly illuminated by God's light. But *only* a few, and they've come when I least expected them . . . kind of crept up on me obliquely. Usually when I go straight to God—as if He were running a complaint department—and righteously pound my fist on the table and demand an answer, I don't get a "suddenly God." (See Isaiah 55. God's ways are not our ways.)

Glimmers of His Glory

Catherine Marshall wrote a book titled *Meeting God at Every Turn*. I wish I could meet God at every turn as Catherine seemed to be able to do. What can happen to me is, I think I'm meeting God, but then I wonder, *Is that really you, God, or just a shadow cast by my own wishful thinking?*

What I have seen is God's *reflected* light. We all have, and it can be wondrous. It reminds me of the time, a year or so ago, when we had a partial solar eclipse in the Midwest—a really good one, in which about eighty percent of the sun was going to be covered by the moon. I love celestial phenomena, rainbows and rings around the moon and the aurora borealis. I almost missed a train one bitter winter morning when I was staring at a sundog, a very rare "mock sun" formed by the refraction of light through ice crystals.

So I wanted to be sure not to miss this eclipse. But how to view it? I tried mirrors, pieces of paper with holes pricked in them—all the tricks—but couldn't see anything. Finally, when the blue began to fade and the sky darkened as the eclipse reached its peak, I had to walk to school to meet Amanda for lunch. I glanced down at the sidewalk—and saw an infinite number of tiny, crescent-shaped sunlets! The street, the lawns, *everything* was covered in shadows shaped like fish scales. Somehow the spaces between the leaves, even the smallest cracks, had created one giant pinhole camera. It was one of the most amazing sights I have ever witnessed, all those little crescents. It wasn't the eclipse itself . . . it was the *reflection* of the eclipse.

Likewise, I've seen God's glory reflected in other people. I've experienced His presence in worship, been aware of His provisions, sensed His guidance in hindsight. *Reflections* of His light.

And maybe that's all any of us can wish for in our earthly sojourn. We dare not look directly at the noonday sun lest we damage our eyes. No mortal may gaze upon God's full glory and live to tell of it.

But just once, wouldn't it be wonderful to be able to look right at the sun and see the black disk of the moon moving over its face, rather than improvising some dumb box or seeing a reflection? Wouldn't it be wonderful to know that surely God was in this place, instead of indulging in guesswork—to come to the garden and have God walk with us and talk with us and tell us we are His own?

To me, that's part of the wonder of C. S. Lewis's *Chronicles of Narnia*—in which ordinary children can encounter the great Aslan, speak to him, touch his fur, even ride on his back. Or, like the disagreeable Eustace in *The Voyage of the Dawn Treader*,[1] be *changed* by him.

For those of us in the real world, though, our awareness of His presence can feel so hit-or-miss, not an ongoing, consistent knowing that transcends moods and temporary circumstances. Claire Cloninger has written about the good-day/bad-day syndrome, where on good days you get up early, have your devotional time, exercise, eat right, work productively, and know God is there. On bad days you oversleep, are crabby, feel fat, and fritter away your time. Where's God then?

We know, too, that God is not some heavenly courier service at our disposal, overnighting us clear instructions about what path we should take. Still, it can all seem so murky and complicated, as if God is making it needlessly difficult for us to get through to Him. Why *can't* we have a "suddenly God" experience?

God is not some heavenly courier service at our disposal, overnighting us clear instructions about what path we should take.

We know He's there. We have His Word on it. He wanted so much to be there—be here—that He made himself one of us. But *how* is He with us in those everyday moments where most of us live? Through prayer, yes, but if we're right-to-the-bone honest, we'll admit that we don't always immediately feel better after praying. Through Scripture, to be sure, but we don't always open the Bible and find the exact verse that speaks to our need. In the normal course of our days, we don't often hear the voice of God from out of the blue, telling us what to do next. We'd like to feel that vibrant assurance that other Christians appear to enjoy . . . but it just isn't always there for us. There's so much in life that doesn't seem very vibrant. It's more like we're blundering on and sort of hoping for the best, hoping that everything will come out all right.

And yet we, too, would touch Aslan's mane.

Letting Go . . . for Good

I want to tell you about some things that happened in my life that made these questions real and urgent. A couple of years ago I really was not liking my life, not liking me, feeling as if long-cherished hopes were hitting dead ends. There was nothing I could clearly identify as the source of these feelings—it was as though I suffered from a vague virus of the soul. I had thought I wanted to work at home, but I was getting restless and bored. A book project I had spent weeks and months on fell through. I had one really awful speaking engagement—I felt as if I had reached nobody. I envied everybody who wasn't me. Prickly misunderstandings with friends ate at me. I now think I was in a mild depression, because I just *felt* so sad and so incapable of rising above the sadness.

I knew, theoretically, that God was there and had a wonderful plan for my life. I had written about all this. Over and over I would pray, "Do something, God. Show me the way. Tell me why I'm so miserable." But God seemed indifferent.

Normally I'm kind of an up-and-down person. This was different, though. I wasn't bouncing back from my downs. The low point came one evening when we went to a concert at church. We had tickets, and we weren't late, yet all the seats were already taken. (The sanctuary had been transformed into a "coffeehouse" for the occasion, so everyone was sitting at tables and, thus, there were fewer places to sit.) For some reason, this hit me wrong—you know how that happens sometimes, like someone is scratching at a raw nerve. It felt like rejection, as irrational as that may sound. Usually I would have handled this better and talked to somebody. Instead, I blinked back tears and grabbed my husband's arm. "Let's go," I muttered. "I'm about to lose it." Once in the car, I sobbed and sobbed.

The incident scared me. It felt out of control, like what I've heard people with clinical depression experience. It was also a turning point. I did not want to be like that. I didn't know *what* I wanted—but I did know I was tired of feeling sad.

I was also tired of trying to think my way out, so tired of strategizing and taking this tack and that tack. Nothing was working. I knew God was there, somewhere amid the emotional clutter of my life, but trying to read God's mind is an exhausting enterprise. I felt as though I'd been trying to lasso the galaxies.

So I turned it over to Him.

That isn't as obvious as it sounds. Of course we turn our concerns over to Him regularly. But we so glibly say, "Let go and let God." I'm not sure that we *do* let go—not really, not as long as we have a scintilla of energy and initiative and hope. We let go . . . and keep taking back, reasserting our control. It's when we're backed into a corner, when we come to the end of that energy, when we feel like a dried-up sponge—that's when Christ comes in and fills up our holes with His living water. That's when we truly understand the meaning of resting in Him.

It's when we're backed into a corner, when we feel like a dried-up sponge, that Christ comes in and fills up our holes with His living water.

I don't remember now exactly what I prayed. It wasn't especially eloquent or quotable (a trap I sometimes fall into when I try to impress God with my talent with words). But I mumbled, in essence, "Lord, I've tried everything. Guess I'm out of ideas. All I know is that I don't want to feel like this anymore. If you have another path for me . . . I'm open to it. I want to do what *you* want me to do. Right now, I'm just . . . plain . . . helpless, and I need you."

And He was there. Not with a "suddenly God" sort of revelation. There was silence, but I hadn't expected anything else. I finished, got up from my knees, and plodded on with my day. He was there . . . not suddenly, but over a long period. Years, actually. His guidance reminded me of those old Burma Shave signs along the roadside—I'm just barely old enough to remember them—that had several words on each sign, and at the end you had a complete message. A little at a time, clue by clue.

There was some backsliding, but I could tell I was healing. I didn't have that panicky sense of flailing about, grabbing for an outstretched hand. I knew what David meant about being brought to a "spacious place." I found myself able to make some decisions, to see things more clearly. And I now have a few clues, clues that might help point the way toward what we all may need to achieve: a mature understanding of how God *does* come to us in the midst of our everyday lives and struggles.

If I had to capture those clues in a few words, here is what I would say:

- God is INCREDIBLY faithful. He can't *not* be faithful. We all can attest to many, many instances where we've seen His faithfulness at work. When we sing "Great Is Thy Faithfulness" in church, I just cry, because the words have such a personal meaning for me. It won't surprise you when I tell you that, during the worst of my depression, God was absolutely there and working in my life. To Him be the glory forever.

   However, His faithfulness isn't just a "there, there" kind of stroking reassurance. It's tough and vigorous and challenging. He wants to work in our lives, but He wants us to cooperate with Him in transforming those lives. He loves us, He believes in us, and so He has given us more responsibility than we sometimes realize. He wants us to figure out some stuff for ourselves, to begin to understand why He has given us the life we have and where He is leading us.

■ He has given us our lives—however mundane they may seem—for a reason. They're the raw material we have to work with, and we can't get anywhere until we take a look at what we have.

■ He wants us to learn patience, to understand that life usually isn't like a revelation in those old biblical epics with the clouds parting and music swelling. I don't mean to say that God *never* works this way, because He has an infinite number of ways of approaching us. But one rather definite clue I got was, *Hang in. I may have created the world in six days, but you're going to take a little longer—the world didn't argue back with me!*

It would sound glib and neat to say that I rapidly recovered from my down period and all the pieces fell into place. Ha! I got out of the immediate emotional crisis, yes. But I'm still working toward understanding, and out of that journey has come this book.

The Long Way Might Be the Best Way

"Suddenly God" appeals to us because there's a part of us that longs to cut to the chase, to have our problems solved and dreams made reality, without any of the boring, grubby, long-term work in between. Like right now, I have a really great idea for a book I want to do when I've finished this one. It's fun to *imagine* working on it, to picture God using it to touch lives. But to get from here . . . the dream of a book . . . to there . . . the book actually published and getting to readers like you, I have to sit down at the computer and plug away over a period of months.

We like to have our problems solved, like in a magazine article that promises "Five Steps to a New You." But life isn't so easily packaged. Think about Scripture itself. In the Old

Testament, the story of Israel's relationship with God shows a "stiff-necked" people who have to keep learning over . . . and over . . . and over again. For every valiant Joshua or faithful Ruth, there's a weak king or lonely prophet warning Israel about her slide toward destruction. In the New Testament, we can, at times, clearly see Jesus' exasperation with His disciples—*Do I have to tell you this again?* Same with Paul, having to devote special attention to quarrelsome young churches, like the body at Corinth, or John, reminding baby Christians about what's really true. The Bible doesn't give five easy steps. God's Word shows His care for people in process, people who fail and get up and try again. They don't always understand God's ways, but they follow Him anyway.

God's Word shows His care for people in process, people who fail and get up and try again. They don't always understand God's ways, but they follow Him anyway.

When I think of my own journey with and toward God, I picture a road made up of those loops like we practiced in second-grade penmanship class. We had orange workbooks that said "Palmer Method" on them, and we did loops and ocean waves endlessly, putting our whole arm into it. (Don't know if it did any good. My handwriting is abysmal.) Anyway, there's the road, with these loopy detours, then I get back on. After my depression, I decided part of the problem was that I needed to be making a steady paycheck. So I started teaching for one of those correspondence writing schools—you've probably seen their ads in magazines. It seemed like a good idea at the time; I could do the work at home and get paid every week.

Well, I found it was taking more and more of my time, time when I could have been writing or simply having a life. I didn't enjoy it *that* much. Eventually it became a perpetual cloud hanging over me, something like a term paper that is never finished. Now I'm not doing it anymore, and I'm much happier.

That was a loopy detour—but, perhaps, a necessary one. I even think that God may have steered me "off-course" to show me what I *am* supposed to be doing.

You may feel right now that your relationship with the Lord is a thing of fits and starts, perplexing detours, unsatisfied longings. Surprise! That's a *good* place to begin. It may even be where He wants you to start—open, trusting Him, seeking Him in humility. And He may respond with a "suddenly God"—just like the Narnians never knew when Aslan would appear. But for sure, He will respond with a "faithfully God."

2

If Only My Real Life Wasn't in the Way!

THIS IS THE FRUSTRATION: You get through your day and wonder if you've REALLY done anything that helped the Kingdom. The feeling can be summed up like this: "If only I didn't have to (fill in the blank) . . . then I could . . ."

I feel guilty because it seems I never get a day to just sit and read God's Word or go volunteer for some needy ministry. I wish my friends and I could have a day to just hang out and talk about books and dreams and the meaning of life, without looking at our watches and going, "Oops! I'm late to pick up Caitlin at preschool!"

I wish I could do something to keep society from falling apart. Just today I was reading an inspiring story in *Christianity Today* about the Rev. Eugene Rivers, a black pastor in Boston who is taking the gospel message to gangbangers and streetwalkers. I worry about the racial divisions in our country. I'd like to help in some way, but I feel like the guy who told Jesus he wanted to follow Him, but first he had to bury his father. I want to be used of God, but first I have to clean the parakeet's cage.

Put it another way: Does it ever happen to you that you're rummaging through a drawer searching for something and you think, *Why don't I get rid of all this junk?* I was looking for a pen one day in the kitchen drawer next to the phone, and to find it I had to go through skillions of old crayons, dried-up markers, outdated address books, expired coupons for stuff we don't use anyway, an old phone book, and just plain stuff that had gotten shoved in the drawer. Yes, it's our "junk" drawer, but this had gotten ridiculous. Things were getting lost and it felt embarrassing, to the point where I'd be ashamed to let anybody see the drawer's contents.

I wondered, *What am I holding on to this stuff for?* So, in a post–New Year's fit of virtue, I cleaned it out. Now I can *invite* friends to look in the drawer: "Need a pen? Need to use a phone book?"

I wish it was that easy to get rid of the rest of the trivia in my life: the ways I waste time, the frittering away of emotional energies, the needless worrying, the treadmill sense of, *Haven't I done this before, over and over?*

Recently I had to copy a bunch of files onto a diskette. There was no easy, streamlined way to do it. Every single time I had to type the command, wait, type the command. I started getting this knot in my stomach. I wanted to scream with boredom. I muttered to myself, "A chimpanzee could do this."

Those endless *if only*'s get the better of me sometimes:

- If only I didn't have to perform meaningless, repetitive busywork.
- If only the laundry stayed clean.
- If only the carpet stayed vacuumed.
- If only the bills stayed paid.
- If only I didn't feel as if I were smothering in trivia!

I remember one night when I was about twelve or thirteen. I had been babysitting for a neighbor and was walking home. It was a warm August night and a huge golden full moon hung in the southeast. The entire sky was bathed in warm blue light; the crickets sang and the grass smelled good, and right then I just felt so *alive*, as if the whole universe was full of promise and the promise was meant for me.

If only I could have that feeling again. Because the promise is still there, still meant for me—only now I know that that promise has a Name.

Being *There* and Not *Here*

We're already talking about our next vacation to Cape Cod, Massachusetts. We go there every summer to visit my mother, who had the decency to move there after my dad passed away several years ago. I've gotten, as Cape people say, "sand in my shoes"—the place draws me like a second home. While much of the rest of the nation broils in ninety-degree heat, we enjoy fresh ocean breezes. We've seen whales, watched the best minor-league baseball in the country through a blanket of fog, paid honor at Pilgrim burial grounds, picked up shells at low tide. One peaceful afternoon Fritz and I enjoyed a wonderful and cheap lunch of lobster rolls, sitting on a roughhewn deck overlooking Provincetown Harbor—one of those "it doesn't get any better than this" moments. I especially like the outer Cape, the "forearm," where it narrows and feels wild and windswept and fragile.

The last time we were there, Fritz and I took a walk around my mother's neighborhood, a hilly section of newer Colonial-style homes carved out of the piney woods that blanket the Cape's interior. We saw several "For Sale" signs. "Wouldn't it be nice if . . ." we said to each other. I actually found myself calculating how much of a down payment we could muster and assessing the merits of the local school system.

We do this wherever we travel, of course—I think a lot of people do. We decide we hate where we live and want to make a change. It happened in L.A., in Atlanta, in Minneapolis. It even happened in Orlando, where every day there were life-endangering lightning storms and where I got attacked by fire ants. (All I was doing was walking across a parking lot. Welcome to Florida.) I tell you, it isn't always rational. Even the Cape doesn't make a whole lot of sense, because it's hard to make a year-round living there (lots of the people who move there are retired), and there are maybe two or three churches I would feel comfortable in.

But it isn't really about moving. It's about possibilities, renewal, the sense of there being more to life. It's *there* and not *here*. *There*, every day is different: Shall we go on a whale watch or visit Concord or just read on the deck? *Here*, the days fall into a pattern: Get husband off to work. Get daughter off to school. Swipe at the housework. Sit at the computer. Drink too much coffee. I fight against a certain drabness of the spirit, a sense of trudging through life. The wheels on the bus go round and round . . . and I don't want to be on the bus, breathing fumes. I want to be on a ship disappearing over the horizon, tasting salt air and singing rousing chanteys. I don't mean to sound ungrateful for the life God has put me in. And I know you aren't either. We have homes, families, work, church, friends, opportunities . . . but it does seem that so often the blessings come with burdens.

The wheels on the bus go round and round . . . and I don't want to be on the bus, breathing fumes. I want to be on a ship disappearing over the horizon, tasting salt air and singing rousing chanteys.

The Burdens of Blessings

I love my house. I remember eight winters ago when we were house hunting with our realtor, a Christian. He showed us a twenties-era brick bungalow on a corner lot in a nice neighborhood. "This is a solid house, great location, well cared for by the previous owners, who lived here fifty years," he said. I didn't want to live in a boring, meat-and-potatoes bungalow. I wanted the quaint little blue cottage I had seen in a neighboring town. But something told me to look again. Once more we went with our realtor—and I had a powerful feeling that this was right. I was able to see past the ugly dining room wallpaper to the friends who would gather around our table, able to envision the bare trees leafed out and blooming. The house felt . . . welcoming. (As for the quaint blue cottage, it got torn down and somebody built a really ugly, oversized, and decidedly unquaint house in its place.)

Our house has welcomed us. It's put us in an excellent school district, among Christian neighbors; it's given me my back porch workspace and a roomy kitchen; it's given my husband a reprieve from exterior painting. It's given us a sense of rootedness we never had before, living in two parsonages and an apartment.

But the house is also a burden. Houses usually are, especially when they're older—all that "character" comes with a cost. (As in, "Lady, it'll cost you about five hunnert dollars to get this done right.") We had the rooms painted before we moved in, and now they need doing again. The bathroom has a window, installed in the days when people took occasional baths instead of daily showers, and the sill is rotting from thousands of hours of water shooting at it. The picturesque landscaping needs constant maintenance. Our closets were built in the days when people had three outfits to their name, and you want to talk about clutter. . . .

I never feel caught up. It's hard to see God through peeling paint, easy to feel resentful of all the stuff that heaps up on us. Sometimes my husband and I will even drive by some treeless, cookie-cutter subdivision and we'll say to each other, "You know, I can sort of see why people buy these. . . ."

Maybe for you it isn't a house, but a job you have to work at that seems to take all your time. You enjoy the people contact, but it doesn't really use your gifts, and you imagine what you could do if only you didn't have to schlepp off to the office every day. Maybe it's kids, and you feel guilty because your best friend homeschools *her* five kids and seems to love being with them twenty-four hours a day—and here you are, counting the days until summer vacation is over and your two are back in school. Maybe you feel like you're smothering in trivia, that you have busyness without purpose and you sense the months and years adding up and what is it all adding up to? Or there's this feeling that you're always sort of improvising, patching, making up half-solutions and not really *changing* anything.

The wheels on the bus go round and round, heading nowhere. If only, if only . . .

That's One Small Step . . .

What I'm coming to see is that maybe there's a *reason* my life is the way it is. Maybe there's a reason I'm not as famous as Catherine Marshall (who also summered on Cape Cod). Maybe God has a purpose for all this mundane stuff. Maybe you and I have to start right here. Maybe our being where we are actually pleases Him.

What I'm coming to see is that maybe there's a reason my life is the way it is.

When I was struggling emotionally a couple of summers ago, I went to my pastor for several counseling sessions. John has an uncanny way of intuitively, instantly grasping a situation. I remember the moment well. It was a torrid

July afternoon, my first visit, and we were sitting in his study with the window air conditioner humming away. After I had rambled through a free-associative recital of my woes, I trailed off and looked at John, wondering if what I said made sense. He said, "You're a creative person. And as a creative person, the gap between the way things are and the way you'd like your life to be is very painful to you, because you so easily see what can be."

Bingo. Hit the nail on the head.

I've realized—not like "suddenly God," but over a long and bumpy road—that if I want to feel as if I'm moving forward, I have to start with my life as it is and not think that my vision for my perfect life will happen by itself. If I want to find God, I have to first look for Him here, and He'll take me to places undreamed of. To find my intended life, I have to begin with my *real* life, which is beginning right now. My real life isn't in the way. It *points* the way.

My real life isn't in the way.
It points the way.

A friend of mine was really struggling with a lot of stuff—lack of money, the demands of young children, the depressing sense that nothing would ever change. In the midst of this, she said something to me that showed real wisdom for someone barely out of her twenties: "I keep thinking my 'real' life is going to start sometime in the future, when everything's solved. But I've realized that this *is* my real life, and I'd better deal with it."

Another woman I know is facing the loss of her longtime position with a Christian publisher. It's a familiar story: The company was acquired by another, larger organization and is moving out of state. Single and in her fifties, she doesn't want to move. Of course she's concerned about her future, but she's taking the attitude, "What is the next thing I'm supposed to do?"

Lina Sandell, the great Swedish composer of such hymns as "Day by Day," told the story of a pendulum. The pendulum complained to the clock face that it was tired of swinging back and forth, thousands of times. That's all it had to look forward to in life—thousands more swings. The clock face counseled the weary pendulum to think of it as one swing at a time.

We can feel like that pendulum, weary and weighted by tedium. If only we didn't have to keep swinging. If only there was more to look forward to.

One of the things I don't want to do in this book is be simplistic. Many of us *are* hemmed in by circumstances, for a variety of reasons. We *do* have to defer some dreams, like moving to Cape Cod. I get really irritated by some of those rah-rah motivational speakers who preach, "Dare to be great! Go for it! Success is at your fingertips! Think big!" It isn't always that easy. As I've gotten older, I've begun to better understand the reasons people don't and can't break out of their boxes, even though it might mean a much better life. The elderly widow may live in a declining neighborhood, but it's been home for forty years. The guy with the boring job might feel "unfulfilled," but he'll accept that over the alternative of unemployment and will find ways to be fulfilled apart from work. Some parents' lives are circumscribed by having to care for disabled children. And some people just don't have that go-for-it, risk-taking personality.

Others do, but they feel trapped by life and don't know where to turn. Which is why I like the idea of starting with the "next thing"—because God honors the small step as well as the giant leap, and a succession of small steps may send you right out on some adventure.

What that "adventure" is, only God knows, but you must believe that it's out there, as sure as the summer moon rises and shines over the land. You, like me, may remember with a wistful pang that sense of youthful hope and wide horizons. Where did that horizon go? When did it narrow?

Well, it's still there, maybe as near as your own backyard. And if only we can look at what God has given us, starting here, we can begin to find Him—even if our junk drawers aren't organized.

Notes

1. New York: HarperCollins Children's Books.

3
God's Come-As-You-Are Party

ARE YOU READY FOR GOD?

God doesn't knock on the door and call, "Are you decent?" He would just as soon walk right in on us, like someone showing up on a Saturday morning when we're still in our robes and the kids are watching cartoons and the cereal boxes are out on the kitchen counter. If, as Tony Campolo has observed, "the Kingdom of God is a party," then it's definitely come-as-you-are.

Think of Moses, who didn't speak very well; of Paul, who, as one account of the time describes him, was a short, bow-legged bald guy; of Peter, who probably wasn't on the guest list for the best Capernaum parties. Of Mary, who was just a kid by our standards. Zaccheus probably didn't think the Lord would actually see him up there in the sycamore tree—let alone inform him that *his* house had been singled out for the honor of a visit from the Master. God didn't wait for any of these folks to "get their act together" before He came knocking.

When I speak to a large group, it helps me to see my audience as individuals, not as an undifferentiated sea of faces. I look out and see all kinds of women. Some are dressed in expensive Shetland sweaters; some in polyester. Some are young moms; others have great-grandchildren. Some have faces shadowed with care; others seem fresh and untroubled. All sizes. All colors.

I really like that. I love getting to know a variety of women. I especially love it that not one of them is perfectly presentable—yet all, in a sense, are presenting themselves to God, through prayer and song and discussion and laughter. A motley group? Sure! And so are we all, whether we're lifting hands in a storefront church or kneeling in a hushed cathedral.

And, says Charles Swindoll, that's what's so marvelous about God—the Almighty, the Father infinitely self-sufficient and all-powerful—who chooses to stoop to you and to me, saying, "Child, I've given you life and breath and brains and spirit. I'm counting on you to do my work on your little planet. Can we do it together?"

He invites us to come now—just as we are, ready or not. Yet so often we find it easier to respond, "No, Lord. I'm not ready or competent. You're God—you do it!"

The Freedom to Fail

One of the hardest things for me to do as a mother is let my daughter do things on her own and thereby learn responsibility. Take, for example, helping her with homework. Lately fractions have been particularly problematic. I know Amanda has learned them at school, but it seems as if every time she has math homework involving fractions she has a sudden attack of amnesia. "I don't get it!" she'll wail. I'll resist the temptation to snap, "Where were you when this was taught, vacationing in Outer Mongolia?" Instead I'll patiently review the principles with her and give her a mini-quiz.

I won't, however, tell her the answer. "You know this stuff," I'll say, trying to keep an even tone in my voice. (How *do* homeschooling parents maintain cordial relations with their offspring?) "What do *you* think? How many halves are in two fourths? Honey, this isn't advanced calculus."

Sometimes she'll try to think. Other times she'll throw her pencil in frustration and exclaim, "I don't know! It's too hard! YOU do it!"

Many of us can fall into the trap of yelling at God, "YOU do it! It's too hard!" Then we wait around for the magic solution to reveal itself. But the more I live life, I'm coming to think that God puts a lot of responsibility on us. Paul speaks of "the glorious liberty of the children of God," and to me that includes the gift of free will and the freedom to fail.

I wonder . . . when God sees us bungling and botching things up, is He ever tempted to step in and say, "Here, let me do it for you"? Yet He shows *greater* love for us by giving us the freedom to fail, to try our wings ourselves, because He knows that only in that freedom is there true growth in Him.

God gives us the freedom to fail, to try our wings ourselves, because He knows that only in that freedom is there true growth in Him.

It's not for me to get into involved discussions about free will versus God's activity in our lives. I think that, like so many biblical questions, it's both/and: faith and works, mercy and judgment, free will and divine leading. But throughout Scripture we see God calling for our response: If you have faith, then this will happen. Draw near to Me, and I will draw near to you. Ask, and you will receive. *You know this stuff. Work with Me here.*

Sure, there are times when, out of compassion for my

tired daughter, I'll tell her the answer. And there are times when God will reveal himself and provide an immediate solution. But we make it easier for Him to use us, just as we are—beginning with our real lives—if we can start sweeping away some of the clutter that separates us from Him.

Clearing a Path to God

It's real insidious the way this junk creeps in. Once I saw a segment on the local news about furnishing a kitchen on a budget. Walking through a Crate & Barrel, the reporter showed how for a little less than five hundred dollars, a single or couple just setting up housekeeping could buy eight place settings of white china, several sets of glasses, a few pots and pans, and simple flatware (but don't skimp on the knives). Everything new and matching and basic. I thought of our kitchen cabinets, with one entire shelf devoted to unwieldy and unused appliances (a salad spinner, a food processor, a juicer) and another cupboard filled solely with refrigerator containers (don't ask for a lot of storage space, you just might get it), and wished *I* was just starting out. Seventeen years of marriage seems to breed seventeen decades of stuff. It sneaks up on you, until one day you realize that to have a proper yard sale, you'd have to rent the Rose Bowl.

The junk that sneaks up on us and separates us from God are those unthinking habits, feelings, responses, beliefs, and behaviors that we accrue through the process of everyday living. It's a blindness to His presence in the ordinary. It's a willingness to settle for less, to live in a safe little complacency. It may even be a fear of truly inviting God in because we don't know what He'll ask of us.

More: Distraction. Busyness. Predictable emotional reactions. Trying to meet others' expectations—or what we *think* are others' expectations—instead of being honest and real and true to ourselves.

This last one is especially challenging for women, even

today, even when many of us know better. I've spoken with a number of pastors' wives who feel burdened by and resentful of the "expectations" of life in a fishbowl. Sometimes the expectations are real, especially in churches with a lot of older saints who fondly recall the days when Mrs. Pastor led the ladies' group, was always ready to pray, taught Sunday school, and invited people in for every Sunday dinner. Sometimes, though, the expectations are self-imposed, born out of a desire to *seem* like the perfect ministry wife.

The "clutter" in our lives blinds us to God's presence in the ordinary.

We can all have misconceptions about what we think *God* expects of us. Pray eloquently. Be available to everyone at all times. Raise children who never rot their brains in front of the TV. Use the "right" spiritual language. Find every passage in Scripture fascinating and life changing.

I want to spend more time on this in the next couple of chapters, because I think it's one of the biggest obstacles to meeting God *just as we are*. When Christ stands at the door and knocks, He wants us to let Him in right away, not stall Him while we run around replacing the *TV Guide* on the coffee table with *Cruden's Complete Concordance*.

You've been there. I've been there. Because . . . it's where we live, a lot of the time. You know, we could go scale some mountain and live on roots and berries for a month and empty ourselves of all these earthly tensions and pretensions, and come back near-paragons. But then what?

Then, we have to return to our families and friends and co-workers, all those unpredictable people whose lives crisscross our own and who help form us and who may not be interested in helping us achieve perfection. Then, we have to go back to the routine: Our employer will not look kindly on "I've been finding God in the wilderness" as an excuse for not reporting for work. Commitments must be met, decisions made. Most inescapably, we have to live with the variables and restrictions of our own personalities.

And that's a *good* thing, because God has no intention of being confined to the mountaintop. You know how sometimes He'll break into our everyday grind and shine His light on the ordinary? Every now and then it happens to all of us—an idea, a conversation, a glimpse of something lovely. Well, God wants to do more than just visit occasionally. He wants to live in our lives *wholly.*

God wants to do more than just visit occasionally. He wants to live in our lives wholly.

The question is, how can we live lives pleasing to God, mindful of His desires for us, aware of His presence—*within* the context of the portion we have been given—while still looking toward that horizon and dreaming of adventures?

Bringing What We Have . . . All of It

Think about where you are now. I don't know where you're reading this. Propped up in bed wearing glasses instead of contacts? Sitting in a line of cars and vans waiting for your kids to get out of school? On your lunch break at work? Here's what I'm doing. I'm writing this on an aging computer on a near-zero winter day, looking out on a snowy landscape. (One of the great things about winter is, there's no yard guilt. You don't have to look out at uncut grass or weedy gardens.) The crows are out flapping around. Somebody just called about speaking in a few months. The Bulls, our beloved basketball team, keep winning and winning. I just got a decent haircut. We have to take Amanda to an orchestra rehearsal tonight; tomorrow night we have to sit on backless gymnasium bleachers through an all-district concert, listening to not only the fifth-graders, like Amanda, but to every other grade as well . . . thus giving new meaning to the term "sacrificial love." Life goes on.

I think about this everyday stuff, and I wonder if there's a "Christian" way to go to a school concert, to drive to work, to walk the dog in subzero weather. (I don't know about that last one. Maybe Christians just use cleaner language as they grumble while leashing up Fido.)

And I think about whether this is a "good time" or a "bad time" for me, and I guess I'd say that right now, things are part okay and part not okay. That's something else I'm learning—life isn't so much peaks and valleys as it's like a forest where magnificent, spreading elms and oaks mingle with boring, sticklike maples (the kind you see planted in new parking lots), and both are interspersed with dead, skeletal trees. In other words, usually the great and the so-so and the bad come mixed together.

But God can use it all, the endless concerts and creaky computers and mixed-up forests. For most of us, our Christian journey is played out not on the mountaintop, but down in the hurly-burly of life. And He *leads* us through that hurly-burly, right toward Him.

You know those maps at the mall that say, "You Are Here"? Whatever your "here" is, whatever your day's been like, whatever the circumstances of your life right as you're reading this, it's from God and He's given it to you for a reason. Think of the mustard seed, the loaves and fishes, the widow's mite. Nothing is too small that it can't be brought before God. We may never have the perfect life or change the world or touch millions, but God invites us to His come-as-you-are party anyway. And He's waiting for us to step through that door and join Him—right now.

4

Where's Everyone Going So Fast?

EVERYBODY ALWAYS THINKS THAT everyone else's devotional life is superior to theirs. Deeper. More meaningful. Certainly more disciplined. What nobody admits is that sometimes, when we come to our morning meeting with God, we have a lot of other things on our mind. This is what can happen: Say you've plopped into your favorite chair, ready for your morning devotions. You have your coffee; or, if you're like certain Southern friends of mine, you have your Coke. All is calm, all is right. Or so you think.

Then you go to prayer: *Father, thank you for—now what idiot would be mowing his lawn at THIS hour? . . . Forgive me for not—oh no, I just realized the carpet cleaners are coming at ten . . . I would especially ask you to work in the situation of—my leg itches . . . And finally, God, I just—is that the baby coughing? . . .*

You try to read your Bible. But somehow your mind keeps wandering. You can't concentrate on Paul's advice or David's adventures. There's just too much to do, too much to worry about. You feel guilty about this, and you apologize to God: Forgive me, Father, for being so distracted. I really do love you, you know. It's just that . . .

43

Just that what?

To paraphrase that old antidrug commercial, the one with the sizzling fried egg: "This is your brain. This is your brain on overload."

Run That By Me Again, God?

I have a friend who, in her late middle years, has been diagnosed with Attention Deficit Disorder (ADD). She described some of her symptoms to me, and, true to form, I began to wonder if *I* have the syndrome. (Whenever I hear about some disease, I think I have it, unless it's prostate problems. Flulike symptoms could actually be one of those deadly jungle viruses for which there is no cure. A headache could well signal one tiny, malignant brain cell.) But there's some justification for my worry about ADD, although my friend said, "You don't have it."

It's hard for me to sit and write for hours. I'll see the mail coming, go get it, decide while I'm up to do some chore around the house, answer the phone, leave the chore half-done, and meanwhile my computer is humming away. I probably should get one of those pretty screen-savers. Distractibility can interfere with my relationships with others. Have you ever had someone talk to you and realized you had only absorbed a fraction of what that person said? How many times have I said to my husband, "I'm sorry, sweetie, could you run that by me again?" It's not that I wasn't listening. I was just . . . wandering. Thinking about what to have for dinner. Trying to finish a project and get it in the mail. Staring at the spot on the kitchen ceiling where the paint is starting to peel around the ventilator fan.

So maybe I don't have ADD. But I have life, which is distraction enough. The problem is, I feel as if I sometimes say to God, "I'm sorry, Lord, I didn't quite catch that. Run that by me again?"

It's enough to make a body long for the life of a hermit. Some time ago I watched a travelogue about Ireland on television. I learned that dozens of beehive-shaped piles of stone dot the Atlantic coast. These "beehives" are actually tiny huts, built by monks around A.D. 700. Here they lived the most rigorous of existences, focused on God and focused on their task of calligraphing those beautiful illuminated manuscripts (and thus helping to preserve Western civilization). I thought, not for the first time, about the contrast between the simplicity of the early ascetics' lives and the cluttered distraction of our environments; between an age when church and government were nearly one and the same and our present darkness.

But some things never change. Even the monks were distracted at times. Occasionally they would scribble comments in the margins of their texts: "Twenty days to Easter Monday and I am cold and tired." "Thin ink, bad vellum, difficult text."

If *they*—without spouses, kids, cars, TV, and phones— were distracted, think about us! No wonder it's hard to concentrate, hard to focus on doing that one great thing, having that one great passion. There's more to worry about, more to keep up with, more balls to juggle (and drop) than ever before. We have to keep track of our children in an increasingly unfriendly world. We have to worry about holding on to our jobs—or worry about finding jobs—in an economy that tosses workers away like used tissue. Many of us aren't getting enough sleep, don't eat right, don't get the exercise that might help our bodies discharge the toxins of stress. We live with noise and pollution and crime and alarming reports about mutant jungle viruses for which there is no known antidote. Sometimes I even wonder if our very brains have been irrevocably altered in some way by the media clamor and the warp-speed tempo of life today.

Have you ever tried to wade through a long and difficult nineteenth-century classic—something by Dickens, say, or perhaps *Moby Dick*—and wondered if people in the olden days were smarter than we are? It's interesting to compare children's books of a few decades ago with today's titles. The older books have smaller print, longer chapters, few or no illustrations. My daughter's American Girls™ books are each about sixty-four pages long with about five chapters and lots of color artwork. Even the instructions on Betty Crocker cake mixes have been simplified and written in larger type. (I don't know how you simplify "Add three eggs," but they've done it.)

There's a prophetic line in a classic old Orson Welles movie, *The Magnificent Ambersons*: "The faster we're carried, the less time we have to care." The observation refers to the changes wrought by the introduction of the automobile, but it could as easily refer to my life, or yours. We can be carried so fast by events and demands that we never stop to *dwell* on anything, to reflect. To care. To "live mindfully," as a wise friend of mine puts it.

We can be carried so fast by events and demands that we never stop to dwell on anything, to reflect. To care.

When our lives are smothered in the clutter of distraction, by the tyranny of the urgent, there's a danger of not only squeezing God into our schedule (the way our hair stylist says, "I can fit you in at five-thirty"), but a deeper risk of thinking superficially about our life with Him—because we're too mentally worn out to think any other way. Just as I take the easy way out when I do housework, straightening what shows and ignoring the rest, I can take the easy way out in examining my beliefs, what really matters to me, what God would have me to do. I parrot familiar Christian lines (saying, "God is in control," when I'm secretly thinking, *As long as He asks me first*). I jump to quick conclusions: *Okay, I prayed about it once. NOW I know what I should do.* I fall into familiar emotional ruts: *I didn't get any phone calls to-day, so that means nobody likes me.* I live reactively, dealing with situations piecemeal rather than looking for a broader pattern.

With such pressures, it seems those monks might have had a good idea, holing up on the seacoast, literally turning their backs on a chaotic continent. In my more pessimistic moments, I wonder if it really is possible to be "in the world but not of the world."

We can—but *only* if we know who we are in that world, serving a Person not of the world.

And to do that, we have to allow ourselves some breathing space.

I won't say I had an idyllic childhood—I didn't, mostly because of my own loneliness and oddness—but I did have one very important thing: space. Ours was the first house on our road, which was gravel and ended at our lot line. All around was pastureland, a creek, a pond, wildflowers, and some newly planted elm trees that did nothing to ease the heat of the sun. It was like *Little House on the Prairie.* (We even had a brush fire one dry fall.) Meadowlarks whistled from the tall grass and occasionally a pheasant would turn up in our yard.

Eventually the road got built up, but it took years. Meanwhile, I spent a lot of time picking flowers, sitting half-hidden by the grass, even, one memorable winter, skating on the frozen creek. The very physical space stirred my imagination and gave my spirit room to roam. I couldn't have put it into words at the time, but I think I was coming close to God—or He to me—during those open and peaceful years.

In Search of Space

It has occurred to me that living in overcrowded, over-urbanized environments may exact some hidden toll on our spirits and may even make it more difficult to connect easily and readily with God. People in Bible times lived close to and in some cases *in* the wilderness. They were familiar with the cry of the wolf, the portents of the sky, the cycle of plowing and planting and harvesting. Martin Luther could draw inspiration from the stars shining through a forest of firs. Even as recently as the early part of this century, young Jack Lewis could look out the windows of his boyhood home near Belfast and see trees and hills and, in the distance, the sea. There's something profoundly reassuring about knowing that space and silence, if you need them, aren't far distant.

Too many of us, however, struggle along without either physical space *or* emotional and spiritual space. We're scheduled and organized, dawn to dusk and beyond, so that our lives are the emotional equivalent of some manicured subdivision—everything ordered and predictable, no delightful little wild places to discover. I know people who pack their days (and their children's days) with commitments, most of which entail driving long distances and keeping in touch with their spouses by beepers and car phones. When they're home, they're toiling away at some chore like sealcoating the driveway.

Maybe you, like me, live in an area where this busyness is almost a status symbol. Once I was at a church board meeting and a woman who had recently taken on a teaching job said jokingly, "Now I can be a real suburbanite and complain about how busy I am." We're among the few families I know who sit on their front porch, who bother to take time to hang laundry out on the line. It just isn't done anymore. How untrendy to have time on one's hands!

I don't mean to imply that busyness is, in and of itself, wrong. There are people—single mothers, for example—who have no choice *but* to maintain a hectic schedule. The work of the world has to get done. Children should have opportunities for recreation and stimulation. And certain personality types actually do better with lots of activity.

But *unexamined* busyness, busyness without depth or meaning or context, busyness that carries us faster and faster, is another story. Without space, without what have been called "margins" to our lives, we become more distracted, more tired, more short-tempered, and more dulled to the things of God.

It isn't only a matter of escape or even respite, because it does no good to stop and smell the roses if you're more interested in growing tomatoes. It won't help you to jump off the treadmill if you have no idea where you want to land.

Without space . . . we become more distracted, more tired, more short-tempered, and more dulled to the things of God.

Lessons From a Rock

In Anne Tyler's novel *Breathing Lessons*,[1] one of the characters, Serena, asks her friend Maggie, "Have you ever stepped outside your own life? . . . What would it be like, I wonder. Just to look around one day and have it all amaze you—where you'd arrived at, who you'd married, what kind of person you'd grown into. Say you suddenly came to while you were—oh, say, out shopping with your daughter—but it was your seven- or eight-year-old self observing all you did. 'Why!' you'd say. 'Can this be me? Driving a car? Taking charge? Nagging some young woman like I knew what I was doing?' "

Step outside your own life. How many of us take the time to do that? To ask ourselves, "Where is all this activity getting me? How am I growing? Am I doing what's really important to me, or am I just reacting to others' expectations?" Or maybe we ask these questions, but never follow up. Or we put barriers in our own path.

A verse in Hebrews holds a clue: "See to it that no one misses the grace of God" (12:15). We can sometimes imagine God's grace as impossible to avoid, like oxygen. "Miss" the grace of God, as one misses a bus or an appointment? The broader context of the passage implies a willful turning from God's grace toward sinful behavior. But I find it sobering to contemplate the possibility that we can miss something very important, simply because we aren't paying attention, because we're stuck in clutter.

This is where we have to cooperate with God. He sends us the clues, but it's up to us to notice them.

God sends us the clues, but it's up to us to notice them.

As midlife has sneaked up on me (I cannot tell a lie), I've felt an increasing urgency to pay attention, to not miss God. In her book *Men in Search of Work*[2] (please, if your husband is suffering through unemployment or a career crisis, read it), my dear friend Diane Eble talks about "developing an attitude of expectation" that God will work in her life. We have to become *attuned* to three things: God and who He is, how He works, and what He has created us to do and be.

I was paying attention when I found my reminder rock on my Cape Cod vacation. It sits atop my work pile like a paperweight. The papers will never blow around because the rock weighs about ten pounds. It's reddish—probably has some quartz in it—and pocked with countless tiny holes and indentations.

I picked up this rock at land's end, on Nauset Beach at Cape Cod. We were there the last evening of our vacation, saying goodbye to the ocean. I was walking barefoot through the surf, which was gentle—that day. I stared out to sea and thought about Thoreau's description of a parade of ships passing on the horizon, a moving forest of masts on their way to the Grand Banks, to the Lesser Antilles, round the Horn in pursuit of the great whales. ("There the ships go to and fro, and the leviathan, which you formed to frolic there"—Psalm 104:26.) I thought about the thousand shipwrecks these shores have seen. I felt a shivery thrill at standing with a whole continent to my back. I did not want to leave.

Then I saw the rock. It lay right at the edge of the water, all by itself, hurled by the sea from somewhere. Perhaps it was there just waiting for me to take it home; I don't know. But I was drawn to it, so I picked it up and began to climb up the bluff. I looked back at the sea one last time, listened to the gulls, smelled the clams frying at the concession stand, thought about the beach grass planted to keep the land from sliding into the water.

Now, a thousand miles west, the rock rests as a reminder that there's more to life than soap scum. There's beauty and silence and simplicity; there's granitelike stability and infinite possibility. And oh, how I long for them. You too?

I can't give you my rock. You'll have to find your own. The interesting thing is, you may not have to travel too far to find it. But first, you have to dig away at the debris that might be hiding it from your sight. After you dig out, you just might find . . . yourself.

Notes

1. New York: Knopf, 1988, p. 53.
2. Grand Rapids, Mich.: Zondervan, 1994.

5
Goodbye, Martha Stewart: Finding Yourself and Pleasing God

OH, MARTHA, MARTHA . . .

It seems that either you love her or you find her terminally annoying. But we'll get to her in a minute. Has it ever happened to you that you're feeling pretty good about something in your life—say, how you're raising your kids—until you read some (usually male) expert's advice and find that, according to him, you've made every possible mistake, and if you keep this up your children will grow up to be serial killers or, worse, talk-show hosts? Have you tried a fruit-only diet recommended by a friend and only lose weight from the exercise you get running to the john? Have you ever been modestly satisfied with your house, until you go to a Bible study at the home of some woman who just redecorated and suddenly your house looks like a pit of squalor by comparison? Or you're starting to be okay with your looks until . . .

I have struggled for years with the burden of comparing myself to others. For instance, I know women who are really good at decorating. They have this knack of placing just the right basket, the right throw pillows, the right little bowl of fruit around. They make wreaths and know how to refinish furniture and re-cover upholstery. I've often wished I could be like that, because my surroundings are important to me and I do care how my house looks. I mean, it's all right, but it lacks those little touches that can really transform an environment. Even my plants just sort of sit there. They don't die, but they don't grow and thrive either, and I can't bring myself to callously throw them away.

I've been dealing with these feelings for some time—let's see, how long have we lived in this house? Eight years now? But I've realized that I am not Martha Stewart, and I really don't want to learn how to make spun-sugar cake decorations or sponge-paint my walls. I don't want to spray perfume on my light bulbs; I have visions of the heat from the lights igniting the alcohol and . . .

Martha Stewart annoys me because she's one of the more visible symbols of the pressure on women to do more, be more, add more fuss and bother to our lives. I mean, if you're good at this stuff, great; but still, I can't help wondering if it's an expenditure of energy that might be better used elsewhere.

I've written before about how I thought I should get a Day-Timer because I thought it looked impressive and would help me organize my life. I know a lot of women who swear by them. I ordered one, it came in the mail, I looked at it, and I thought, *This doesn't fit my life.* I know quite a few women who homeschool. I've seriously considered the option, but it wouldn't fit my daughter, and it wouldn't fit my work schedule.

I've decided I'm tired of worrying about what I'm not. I think I'd rather concentrate on pleasing God—starting with who I am.

This sounds easy, in theory. "I did it my way" and all that. But if you listened to some experts, you'd think we were all supposed to fit in some one-size-fits-all mold: *This* is the way to discipline your children. *This* is the way to conduct your spiritual life. *This* is the way to manage your time. And what happens is that we're all going around feeling guilty, thinking we're the only ones who are messing up, not realizing that nobody else fits the mold either. "One-size-fits-all" doesn't work for pantyhose and it doesn't work in life. And, if you look at Scripture, you see that the advice is really quite simple: Do justice and love mercy and walk humbly with God. Love God and love your neighbor. Clothe yourself in patience and kindness. Forgive. Obey. Worship and glorify the Holy One.

"One-size-fits-all" doesn't work for pantyhose and it doesn't work in life.

It's more than the Martha Stewart how-to-be-a-successful-woman thing. A lot of people have been hurt by the church's busybody tendency to tell others how to run their lives. I've seen judgment masked as "accountability," criticism masked as "speaking the truth in love." And certainly the Christian community, most particularly the local church, is obliged to hold its members to godly standards. But is it "godly" when a woman feels uncomfortable in her neighborhood Bible study because everyone comes dressed to the nines and she can't afford new clothes? Is it godly when a woman senses rejection from others in her church because she and her husband are childless—and not by choice? Is it godly when a woman senses others' judgment for quitting her job because, as everyone "knows," the family could sure use the money? These are all real examples, by the way. You can probably add your own.

Why I've Given Up Spanking

I've learned to be very careful before judging someone else's marriage, the way she raises her kids, whether she works outside the home or not, what she spends her money on—because *she* is not *me*. For example, I may think that someone else really shouldn't buy her kids' clothes from The Gap because the family is tight for money. I heard Dr. Haddon Robinson, the great preacher and professor, say in a radio interview, "To understand someone you have to see not just where they are, but where they've come from." What I may not know is that this woman was the youngest of five and always wore hand-me-downs growing up, and it gives her pleasure to see her children in new clothes, and she's economizing elsewhere. Someone might wonder why I don't spank my kid when she acts up. What *that* person doesn't know, and what I've learned through hard experience, is that spanking doesn't work with Amanda. (Bribing does.)

Seriously . . . if you're a mother, you know how frustrating parenting can be. For several years I have had an uphill battle encouraging my daughter to sit and read quietly—as I thought all children "should" do. I began to worry that she would become an academic also-ran. Then we went to a natural history museum with all kinds of hands-on activities geared for children. It was a revelation to watch Amanda race from one thing to another, eagerly writing down her findings on the question sheet provided, pushing buttons and picking up objects. She was learning . . . and loving it.

When Amanda started fourth grade, the teacher assigned homework four nights out of the week. This was a huge adjustment for her—and us. My husband would helpfully say things like, "Why don't they let kids be kids? When *I* was her age, all the homework I ever had was to go pick a milkweed pod and bring it to class."

"When you were her age, Alaska was still a territory, Elizabeth Taylor was only on her third husband, and the Dodgers were in Brooklyn," I would respond. Besides, the school had decreed homework, so homework it was. I entertained notions of making Amanda a nice, quiet workspace at the desk in her bedroom. I discovered, however, that *she* preferred to work at the dining room table, smack dab in the middle of household distractions. And, almost always, her work was flawless.

I couldn't figure this out until I saw an educational psychologist on TV (where else?) talking about learning styles. She identified three types—including the "kinesthetic" (or hands-on!) type who works better among people and noise. Her description of the kinesthetic learner fit Amanda almost perfectly. Knowing this has saved many tearful arguments. I still wish she'd read more, but I realize she is learning in her own way—as God created her.

Even advice on practicing the spiritual life, once you get past the overarching requirements of Scripture (worship, prayer, caring for the needs of others), has to be adapted to who we are, and I think God understands; after all, He's the One who made us with such diversity. We all need to feed our spirits, but maybe not all with the same sort of nourishment. You may feel guilty because you've tried to stumble your way through *Pilgrim's Progress*—the original version, not some of the dumbed-down editions that have come out in recent years—and encountered your own Hill of Difficulty in the seventeenth-century language. Guess what? Devotional classics are *hard*! I know people who love to read in solitude, poring over the early church fathers, but I also know people who get restless sitting still too long. (They must be kinesthetic learners.) Our friend Tom the Handyman has said he's much happier when he has something physical to *do* at church—standing and ushering, serving Communion. For him, the best kind of spiritual retreat probably happens when he's perched on top of a roof, hammering shingles as he helps build a house on a youth missions trip to Appalachia. I've heard Bill Hybels, pastor of the Willow Creek megachurch outside Chicago, say that when he has his morning devotions, he has to write his prayers in his journal and *then* say them to God—otherwise his mind wanders too much.

God can use Tom—I've seen it. God can use Amanda— I've sensed it ever since she was born. God certainly has used Bill Hybels. God can use you. God uses all kinds of un-ready and unlikely people.

But we help Him along when we begin to move toward authenticity—not just a sense of who we aren't, but who we are; a sense of what's essential for us.

Are You Satisfied or Sated?

There are dozens of books and seminars and tests that can help you figure out your personality type, your voca-tional preferences, and so forth. It's become a veritable cot-tage industry in recent years. Some of the more detailed as-sessments are really helpful, because they can guide you toward understanding yourself and those around you.

But we have to begin with listening to ourselves, because as we do that we might also heed what God is trying to tell us.

We need to pay attention to those times when every-thing's clicking on all cylinders. When the writing's going well I feel that spark; when I sense a connection while speaking to a group I feel it. It happens to me when I'm out in my garden on a nice day; when I cook a meal for friends— I really love bustling about the kitchen; when my husband and I get into some rambling conversation that covers everything from childhood memories to why some churches grow; when I watch my daughter play park-district basket-ball. It can happen when I'm reading a book and feel a close connection to the author, like she's been through what I'm going through. It happens a lot when I get outside myself and do something to help someone else. And it can happen when I'm thinking or talking about something and I stumble upon some insight that feels really, really true, as if God has shown it to me.

I've also noticed that the best of these feelings are ener-gizing. They make me want to do *more*. It's as if I've con-nected myself to the current of God's pleasure. I think that may be the secret of some extraordinarily busy people—for example, Christian leaders who preach and write books and run institutions and seem to have a million demands on their time. Sure, they get tired, but they're energized by their work. They're doing what God wants them to do.

Conversely, there are those things that can make me feel dull and sluggish, sated but not satisfied (think about the way you feel after too many potato chips). It's not a *bad* feeling, but sort of blah and definitely not energizing. It's a taking in, a *consuming* instead of creating. Too much TV will do that. Too much running around on errands. Too long a time on the same routine without a break. Too much crabbiness and not enough love. To me, feelings like that signal a need to reconnect with God's pleasure—with Him. This isn't just some suspect subjectivism. Think about how your body tells you what's wrong. If you're thirsty, you need to drink (and by the time you feel the thirst, you're probably already slightly dehydrated). If you start getting that curious hot-but-chilled sensation, you should take your temperature. And so on. In the same way, we need to learn to trust these recurrent signals of our souls, just as we might wonder if a recurring dream is trying to tell us something.

We need to learn to trust these recurrent signals of our souls, just as we might wonder if a recurring dream is trying to tell us something.

The interesting thing to me is that as I read my list of what energizes me and gives me that "click" of pleasure— even joy—I realize that the things that count the most to me have very little to do with having a lot of money or prestige or material things. I always *think* I would like to have more money, but when I look at what really satisfies. . . . it's family and friendships and books and ideas, church and ministry and God's creation. And maybe a good dog. (Okay, and an occasional trip to Starbucks.)

What satisfies you, gives you that spark? Are you giving enough time to these things, these people, these pursuits? I know I don't always. Everybody always laments their busyness, but are we looking seriously enough at what we're spending time and energy and money and emotion on?

We all spend way too much time on stuff that doesn't really matter that much to us. I remember once being somewhat shocked when a man I respect a great deal told me he didn't read the newspaper or watch the news on TV. I thought, *But don't you want to be informed?* Yet this man heads up a large Christian organization. He has a family. He needs to spend time in prayer and reflection, and he needs to rest. Because of that, he's learned to steward his time and energies with a sort of disciplined economy, and I admire that and am trying to learn from his example, to live at least somewhat mindful of what matters.

There isn't always a quick answer—it goes back to that "one-size-fits-nobody" idea. What's a waste of effort for me might nurture you, and vice versa. And the Bible doesn't always give clear instruction. But I keep going back to Paul's advice to the Philippians to "think on these things." Pray for wisdom in the face of today's glut of choices. Seek *first* the Kingdom of God (Matthew 6:33). Don't do something just because you think it's expected. Make choices that somehow, some way, advance God's Kingdom.

I can't make up my mind about a new computer, for example. Mine is old by today's standards. On the one hand, it does one thing—word processing—very well. On the other, it isn't equipped to run CD-ROM or the computer games (some of them very creative and educational) that Amanda wants. I can't access the World Wide Web with all those pretty pictures. I'd love to get e-mail. But would such an instrument complicate my life, be an expensive waste of time? Would I spend my working hours hanging out in those chat rooms rather than meeting important deadlines? Would Amanda stumble upon something seamy out in cyberspace? Would it raise our already-scary electric bill? Would I be yielding to the temptations of the consumer culture? Or could we connect with other Christians? Would my professional ministry be enhanced?

You see the dilemma. What I'll probably wind up doing is talking to Christians I trust who have these new toys, getting their counsel. Then I'll wait until prices come down, which they're supposed to do, and see about a Macintosh. (And then I'll have the problem of what to do with my faithful old friend. Catherine Booth and Susannah Wesley never faced these challenges.)

I always think I would like to have more money, but when I look at what really satisfies . . . it's family and friendships and books and ideas, church and ministry and God's creation.

Perhaps it's enough that I'm at least trying to be intentional. Maybe that's all any of us can do, especially in those areas where Scripture doesn't give specific guidance. Maybe all we can do is pray that we become more like Christ, be filled with more of Him and less of us—however God chooses to make that happen.

It helps to look to models, people who inspire you in this search for truthful living. When the recent movie *Little Women* came out, my daughter and I went to see it, and we loved it. It sent us back to read (or, in my case, re-re-re-read) the original. We also started reading everything we could find about Louisa May Alcott and visited the home in Massachusetts where she wrote the book. I've found in Louisa—I can't call her anything else—a kindred soul, a woman of courage and humor who struggled with her temper, questioned the conventions of the day, and sometimes became discouraged about her writing. She never owned a real desk but often wrote with her black case balanced across her lap. In an era of useless ornamentation, Louisa was the real, unvarnished article. She knew herself, and she relied on God to keep her path straight and true.

What is best and truest for you? Can you trust yourself to seek it, to listen to yourself, to heed what God may be saying to you, regardless of anyone else's expectations? Can you strip away the nonessentials, kick away the clutter?

One Mission or Many?

Now that I've got you all excited, I want to offer a caution. Many of us think that there's the "One Great Thing" that God is calling us to, some Everest of a life purpose: Follow every rainbow till you find your dream! This may be true for Mother Teresa and a few other souls who have a single-minded commitment to, say, music or art or science or teaching. But most of us are probably called to more than one life mission. Louisa devoted as much energy to caring for her family as she did to her writing. I know I'm called to the work I do, but that work can take many forms. I also know that I share a purpose with my husband in building a life and growing a child together.

These purposes can sometimes conflict—Louisa periodically found it necessary to rent a place in Boston to live away from her family and write in solitude. There are times I have to stop in mid-chapter to start dinner. At such times we can feel ourselves beset by cluttery demands and long for that clear summons to the mountaintop.

Here again, though, we underestimate God. (Of course

we do—how could we *overestimate* the Almighty?) Remember that we're starting where we are, and that God uses everything. Up to a point, the tension of balancing competing demands can actually energize us. The interplay between work and relationships, solitude and companionship, structure and leisure is probably healthy. But finding that ideal balance . . . well, I think we're all working on it.

You know that saying, "Be patient, God isn't finished with me yet"? I like that. We are God's workmanship, but we're all works in progress. I may want to be as stripped down as a spare eighteenth-century room, but I'm still under construction, and so are you. Purposes can and do change. Circumstances change. God may send us a surprise—or throw us a curve. And, as we shall see, we need to be ready.

6
Getting Back on Track
When You Feel Derailed

ALL RIGHT. You've figured out your personality type, your gifts, your priorities. Great. Important step. Now, guess what happens? Yep—some glitch. Murphy was right.

Much of life is not controllable. That's my quarrel with these books and seminars that seem to say, "Just figure yourself out, and your life will fall into place." Sometimes life doesn't fall into place; it falls into pieces. Your problem may be that you know very well what's important to you, but somehow your family, your boss, and your balky car haven't gotten the message. You've finally made the time to get away by yourself at a friend's lakeside cottage, and on the way there your car breaks a belt and you're forced to spend the night in Upper Armpit while it gets fixed.

I once heard someone say that Jesus' life, as recounted in the Gospels, is mostly a story of interruptions and His response to those interruptions. Jesus did not wake up each morning and say, "Okay, Peter, let's go over the appointment schedule." Yes, He had a clear sense of His earthly mission, and I'm all in favor of each of us—called to be like Christ—knowing what our mission is, being able to answer those why-are-we-here questions.

But a *mission* is different from an *agenda*. Think of how many of the Lord's encounters went something like this: "As Jesus started on his way, a man ran up to him and fell on his knees before him. 'Good teacher,' he asked, 'what must I do to inherit eternal life?' " (Mark 10:17). Jesus was always being stopped by people who needed Him.

> *Your problem may be that you know very well what's important to you, but somehow your family, your boss, and your balky car haven't gotten the message.*

We aren't Jesus. Crowds don't gather wherever we go. However, as Christians we are to look to Him as our beacon. As I reminded my daughter the other night—she was saying something critical about a friend of hers, and I admonished her with, "Jesus wouldn't talk like that." Her comeback: "No offense, Mom, but, well, Jesus was perfect." (Sometimes I think parenting is like throwing suction darts at the ceiling and hoping a few stick.)

But we adults can sometimes think the same thing: Jesus was sinless, so how can I ever be "Christlike"? Yet He was also fully human, minus the sin. Maybe there were times He was tired and would rather not have been interrupted. Scripture doesn't really say, but I think it's possible. But He always used these encounters as a means to draw people closer to the Father, to teach something about the Kingdom.

So, too, life is always waylaying us in one sense or another. There will be times you might have to teach toddler Sunday school whether you're "led" to or not. A friend might call, desperately needing your help. You might find yourself pregnant with twins—or just pregnant. Your company re-

organizes, and suddenly you're out of a job. You're expect-
ing out-of-town guests for the holidays and your boss drops
a major project in your lap and says, "Finish this by the New
Year." Several major appliances (probably conspiring via
your house current) decide to give up the ghost simultane-
ously. Your mother falls and breaks her hip and the doctors
say she can't live by herself anymore.

I don't deal with changes from the plan very well. Never
have. I remember when I was ten or eleven, my mother was
going to take my best friend, Sue, and me to downtown Chicago for lunch at a nice restaurant. At the last minute my
friend's mother called and asked if Sue could bring her
cousin, who had come to town unexpectedly. I had been
looking forward to the occasion for some time, the way kids
do, and I was really upset. "Why does her creepy cousin have
to come? That ruins everything. Say no!" I hissed to my
mother, who of course said cheerfully into the phone, "Why,
sure, Jean. No problem."

Sue's cousin turned out to be a nice girl about our age
named Donna, and we all had a good time. I think I man-
aged not to sulk. But I'll never forget the sense of near-
betrayal I felt: *This wasn't the way it was supposed to be!*

Granted, I may be an extreme example of uptight rigidity. (For those of you familiar with personality-type theory,
you may have already guessed that I'm a J. In other words,
I like the sense of loose ends tied up, everything accounted
for, life going according to plan . . . okay, uptight rigidity.)
But even the most easygoing, take-it-as-it-comes types
among us probably carry around mental snapshots of "The
Way It's Supposed to Be." I once had a pastor who spoke in
this gravelly Boston accent. One of his favorite sermonic
phrases was, "That's the way things ahh." He and his wife
had lost a daughter to cystic fibrosis, and their son also had
the disease, so he knew something about the way things are
. . . and how God gets us through.

Often, though, when we're confronted with the interruptions and derailments of real life, we're inclined to respond

with a variant of, *But, God, this wasn't in the program! This wasn't how it was supposed to be! I was supposed to stay married! My parents were supposed to live till ninety and die in their beds! My husband was supposed to keep the same job forever!* Even, *This was supposed to be my one day to myself, and my in-laws just called from the interstate rest stop outside of town and they're on their way!*

Even the most easygoing, take-it-as-it-comes types among us probably carry around mental snapshots of "The Way It's Supposed to Be."

Normal reactions. And, as we've already observed, it's constructive to have a sense of who you are and where you're going. But all the plans and designs and lists and goals in the world can't buffet us against life's unpredictabilities. In the last year alone, for example, my close circle of family and friends has been shaken by divorce, cancer, and other changes. You can probably name some similar upheavals among those you're close to. Everybody can.

When It's Least Expected . . .

Just the ordinary course of life can knock us for a loop. One day our kid is . . . well, a kid, fairly predictable and easy to handle. The next (or so it seems) she's an oily-haired preadolescent who takes half-hour showers and surprises you by suddenly deciding she wants to clean out her closet. We visit our parents and notice something we'd rather not see: They're getting old. We get that long-dreamed-of work opportunity, and we find it's almost too much to handle.

Kids grow up. Parents age. Life happens. It becomes clear, then, that if we aren't able to roll with the punches, life is going to flatten us. This does not mean that we abandon all hope of any cohesion and context in our lives and just sort of careen from one thing to the next. We can bring meaning out of the chaos.

God may send us these challenges for a reason—to teach us or stretch us or remind us who's really in charge around here. I suspect, however, that He doesn't want us to waste time wailing about how things didn't work out the way we planned.

Let's say, for example, that you and your siblings have determined that if Mom is to continue living independently, she's going to need help. As the person who lives closest to her, it's fallen to you to juggle your work and your family and drive an hour each way several times a week to help her with cooking and cleaning and shopping and finances. It isn't easy—some days it's a big headache—but in the process you realize that you haven't spent this much time alone with your mother in years, and you're thankful for the opportunity to reconnect.

Some of these upheavals can help give us a sense of *proportion*. Too many women, and I include myself, have a tendency to dramatize everything, to blow things up into huge crises. The stove broke down, and isn't that typical of my life, everything falling apart, I think machines hate me, and we're already broke, and woe is me. . . . No. It's important to be able to pick apart problems—not to view them as some vast, malignant ball of wax—and ask ourselves, "What's really happened here?" What's happened in the case of the stove is that an appliance that functioned faithfully for twenty years came to the end of its useful life, as appliances do, and, because one can't do without a stove, one will have to go out to Sears or wherever and purchase a new model. As Robert Fulghum has said, we have to learn to distinguish between problems and inconveniences, and there are many interruptions that fall into the latter category.

Upheavals can teach us humility and an openness to God's working. I have a feeling that many of us, especially those of us who have been around the church for a long time, have preconceived and even arrogant notions about how God *should* work. Who He touches. Who He uses. It's a prideful sort of clutter that can obscure our vision of the Almighty. Many of us are very good at controlling our environment. A "good day" for us is a day when we've gotten everything done we set out to do. We take pride in our achievements, our organization, our ability to execute our plans to match the vision. Too often my prayers are a variant of, "Lord, help me to get everything done today." What I, perhaps, should be praying is, "Lord, show me your face today."

It's important to be able to pick apart problems—not to view them as some vast, malignant ball of wax—and ask ourselves, "What's really happened here?"

I have one friend who does spontaneity very well. She's likely to show up at my door out of the blue, saying, "I was just driving by on the way back from the dentist and thought I'd drop by. If this isn't a good time . . ." A "good time" for me to receive callers is when there are no dishes in the sink and the beds are made and the newspaper clutter is out to the recycling bin and I'm dressed, preferably with mascara on. (Parenthetical statistic here: Some organization polled a representative sampling of women, asking, "If you had to choose only *one* piece of makeup to wear, what would it be?" Mascara won, hands—or eyelashes—down.)

Unexpected visitors unsettle me. (Gosh, I'm sounding

like a lot of fun.) I'm not sure I radiate the gift of hospitality when my friend comes by, and I feel guilty about it.

But one time this friend stopped by and I was coming down with some fluish thing. It was cold, I was in my robe, and I peered out of the front door like an elderly lady in a crime-ridden neighborhood, and said, "I'm sick." So she went away.

Later I thought, *I COULD have invited her in instead of making her stand outside in the cold. I'm not THAT sick—she could have waited five minutes while I got dressed. She doesn't care how I look or how my house looks.* Maybe I missed an opportunity.

Too often my prayers are a variant of, "Lord, help me to get everything done today." What I, perhaps, should be praying is, "Lord, show me your face today."

The next time she came by, a few months later, I was dressed and reasonably healthy, but in the middle of work. Nevertheless, I thought, *Who knows what God may have in mind with Charlene's stopping by? Maybe there's no great purpose, maybe just one heart reaching out to another. But if I say I'm busy, I'll never find out.* I let myself be interrupted; I stepped a bit away from my neat, orderly vision for my life; and I think I grew a bit in the process.

Painful Steps

Sometimes, of course, there is no neat lesson to be drawn. Some things happen to us that seem chaotic, purposeless, hurtful. There's a lot of hard stuff that has to do

71

with faithfulness and trust and just plain hanging in there, clinging to Jesus, taking it "step by step," as the chorus goes.

So far, the worst thing that has ever happened to me was watching my dad get sick and languish in a hospital and finally pass away. Five years have passed and I still have memories that are burned into my brain like horrible photo negatives, memories that still make me cry. Here's Dad, having to hold on to the banister because there's something wrong in his brain that makes him dizzy. He was coming down to have some tapioca, the last thing I ever cooked for him. Here's Dad, lying on the gurney post-surgery, giving the thumbs-up sign. Here's the sound of the ventilator going wheeze, wheeze. Here are the smells of the hospital, antiseptic and plastic furniture and processed air and lurking staphylococcus bacilli. Here am I, alone with my dad shortly after he left us . . . but here, I draw the curtain.

I can't really say I learned some "lesson" from losing my dad. Oh, I had to grow up; suddenly the world felt a little less safe. As I shared in *Sometimes I Feel Like Running Away From Home*, I began to take a hard look at my life and what I really wanted.

But I'd rather have Dad back.

Still, as much as I miss him and as awful as those months were, I can look back and say, *With God's grace, I got through*. I felt alone a lot of the time; grief is a terribly private thing that not even the dearest friend or spouse can assuage. I still had to show up for work most days, and it was hard to concentrate. Sometimes it even hurt too much to pray. But there I was, one foot, other foot, day in, day out, hanging on to God almost without knowing it.

Or, perhaps I should say, He was hanging on to me.

In the end, it's all we have. He's all we have. And whether you're dealing with an annoyance or a true grief, you *must* know that God is right there with you. You may even feel the touch of His hand—and the drop of His tears.

The way it's supposed to be? You and me and all of us, trusting in the Lord, resting in His sufficiency, confident of

His purposes for us. There's a hymn we occasionally sing in church, and I can only think of a few words from it, but they're enough: "Ask me what great thing I know . . . Jesus Christ, the crucified."

7

How Is Sin Like Carpet Mites?

"WHY DO I NEVER LEARN?"

Have you ever groaned that sentiment to a friend? As in, "I volunteered to head up the VBS program this summer. Why do I never learn?" As in, "I had a deadline to get this work done and I procrastinated AGAIN and now I'm going to have to stay up until two. Why do I never. . . ?" Or, more seriously, "I know I have to stop snapping at my husband. We had another fight and I feel awful. Why. . . ?"

And so on. You know the litany. I myself can recite it by heart. For instance, I've written before about learning how to say no to requests for your time. But I've started to realize that for me, it isn't a matter of saying yes. I *offer* even when nobody is asking. I *invent* reasons to overbook myself. One November our adult-ministries board was planning the Advent schedule. One Sunday was blank. What were we going to do? "I know!" I exclaimed fecklessly. "I'll write a play."

And cast the play. And run off scripts. And rehearse. And make a dozen calls about rehearsing.

It didn't matter that I also had to leave town on a five-day business trip, that I was running the school book fair, hosting Thanksgiving dinner, and giving my daughter a birthday party. I had already filled my plate so that stuff was starting to fall off the side. I love sanctuary drama. I had the germ of an idea. So there I was, adding another commitment.

Sometimes I can conquer my overcommitment. I keep my mouth shut when somebody at church or school asks for help. I focus on the two or three most important claims on my life. Other times I cheerily step forward, oblivious to the fact that in doing so I'm risking falling flat on my face.

Another area of struggle for me is putting things off. (I know what you're thinking—why does a procrastinator overbook herself? There's probably some convoluted psychological connection between the two.) It isn't just that I put off unpleasant tasks like telling my husband I bought something from a door-to-door salesman. (When this happens I feel like Lucy Ricardo, bawling while Ricky says, "Loo-see, you better 'splain.") I put off things like calling to make a hair appointment. I put off writing an article until days before it's due. Why? I don't know. I'm *trying* to do better . . . but often it's like one of those cartoons where Mickey Mouse has a little mouse angel whispering in one ear and a little mouse demon in the other.

At these times I wonder, *What is it with me? I know the tricks. I read self-help articles. I understand some of the psychological roots of these problems. I've delved into my childhood. Certainly I know the Scriptures. And STILL I do battle.*

But really, it's not the overcommitment problem, or the procrastination problem, or the crabby problem. It's the over-and-over problem.

Most of us don't have a *lot* of struggles. What we have are a handful of recurring struggles, issues that keep coming up, hooking us, dragging us down. For you it may be low self-esteem, or whining, or a desire to control, or laziness. You think you've licked it, and maybe, for a few months, you have. And then . . . I read these articles about how some woman found a handy-dandy solution to one of these problems, and now her life is so easy, and I think cynically, *Just wait, sister.*

> *Most of us don't have a lot of struggles. What we have are a handful of recurring struggles.*

So Why Are We Still Stuck?

We all live with gaps between the way things are in our everyday life and the way we would like to move in our Christian life. The larger the gap becomes, the more discouraged we can get . . . and the more distant God seems. Life in Christ is about transformation. Paul spends a lot of time talking about the old nature versus the new nature: *Then* I did such-and-such, *but now* I don't. So we can ask ourselves, "If I'm a Christian, why do I still get stuck?"

Despite the expectation of a new life, a new nature, promised to us as Christians, we feel we are not moving forward, growing, making significant changes that *stay that way*. We hope to be like a room that stays cleaned once and for all. Instead, here we are, still stuck in the dust and the clutter.

Speaking of dust, my husband once thought about selling air purifiers (probably to gullible housewives like me). He even attended training sessions where the sales reps learned all about the product. He came home full of such edifying tidbits as, "Did you know that when you step on carpets, you're walking in flakes of dead skin that fall off of our bodies? And that invisible mites eat these flakes, and ordinary vacuum cleaners don't get rid of them? Oh, could I have some more potatoes?" Yum. *Bon appetit.*

Some of the problems in our lives are like dust mites, or

the airborne mold allergens that give so many people sinus headaches. One summer the mold count in our area was something like 10,000 something per something—spores per cubic foot, let's say. I know people who really suffer from high mold counts. They get sinus headaches, runny noses, red eyes. And there isn't a whole lot they can do about it. Nobody has yet invented a machine that sucks the mold out of the air. If you have air, you have mold. And mites.

In the same way, if you're human, you have problems. Recurring ones.

How Our Gifts Become Our Faults

A few years back I had the privilege of interviewing Bill and Gloria Gaither. Both were intense, insightful, candid. One of the things Gloria said made a whole lot of sense— one of those "so *that's* why" comments that puts things into perspective. She said, "My gift is my fault."

In other words, our good traits can produce bad fruit. Perfectionism, for example, can be an asset if it pushes us to strive for excellence. But it can also make a person driven, obsessive, never satisfied. Sometimes perfectionism keeps us from trying anything because we're afraid of doing less than our best. (So that's why I procrastinate. I just want to do a good job!)

Multiple talents can be a blessing—or a curse. I once knew a woman who was gifted with a great variety of abilities and interests. She was probably brilliant. But you know what happened? That woman bounced from job to job. She never finished anything because something else would engage her curiosity and off she went, like a preschooler wandering from toy to toy.

This gift/fault dichotomy sharply reveals what author Jerry Bridges calls the division between our "Christ side" and our human, or fallen, side. The side of me that is Christ is energetic, involved, eager to use my talents to help others and live in a healthy balance between work, family, and outside commitments. The side of me that is fallen overbooks myself—possibly because I want to be applauded for how many balls I can keep juggling—then starts tripping over those very same balls as they go careening out of my control.

When we surrender to Christ, we don't surrender our personalities. Those are God-given. If you were outgoing before you became a Christian, you'll still be outgoing afterward. I suspect that when I received Christ, there were people who were worried that I would "change"—lose my sense of humor, become pious and dull. (What does this say about how we Christians sometimes present ourselves to the world? For that matter, what does this say about the world?)

Well . . . I have changed; or, more accurately, *been* changed, and completely for the better. And I don't think I'm dull!

God made you the way you are for a reason, a purpose—His purpose. With that, though, comes a challenge. He might say to me: "Child, I have bestowed on you my gifts of sensitivity, creativity, imagination. But it is up to you whether you use those gifts to my glory—or fritter them away in worry and hypersensitivity and too much idle dreaming." We have the responsibility to monitor ourselves—or to seek the counsel of trusted friends. Remember how in *Little Women* Jo started writing trashy stories, until Professor Bhaer's concern made her realize that she was wasting, and even corrupting, her talent?

There are other reasons we fall into the same emotional and behavioral ruts over and over again. Laziness, fear of change, simple habit, behaviors we picked up in childhood—all these things work against lasting transformation. Then there's life itself, which keeps throwing up roadblocks—sickness, unforeseen expenses, job upheavals. We think, *I'm trying. I have good intentions. But how can I make any progress against these things over which I feel I have no control?*

The Things We *Can* Control

I want to tell you about a problem I actually solved. (I say that with bated breath because statements like that can come back to haunt you. Okay, call it a lesson I actually learned.) Anyway, here's what happened. My husband and I have periodically wrestled with financial problems. Nothing like some people. But it seemed that there was just never enough, and we couldn't see a time when there *would* be enough. Some nights I would lie awake—you know how that is—and listen to what I fancied was the distant howling of the wolf slinking toward our door. During the day I would be busy, occupied in something, feeling pretty good, when the thought would break in: *But we don't have enough money.*

It was awful. Most important, it wasn't *changing* anything.

So I decided to stop agonizing, get off the worry treadmill. Part of our financial struggle stemmed from choices we had made, and we had to live with the consequences of those choices. Part of it stemmed from things we had no control over. I could, however, control my *attitude.*

It was almost like intentional denial. Sometimes I would just refuse to think about money. (This sometimes drove my husband crazy, but he conceded the wisdom of the strategy, if only because I was easier to live with.) I dealt with the issues when I had to—but not before. I won't say our money problems went away, but by not worrying I saved mental energy that was better applied to calm, clear-headed planning with my husband.

Trust me, this was a huge step because I like to worry. My mind, periscopelike, is always scanning the horizon of my life, on the lookout for worry targets. If there's nothing to worry about, I worry that there's . . . well, you get the idea. But more than liking worry, I hate feeling stupid, like I'm wasting my mind on pointless stuff. I knew I had a choice:

to waste, or to channel my energies in more productive directions.

We *always* have a choice over our attitude. No matter what our outward circumstances are, we can choose how to respond. God has placed that choice in our hands.

Some time ago I watched a segment on one of those TV news magazine shows. It told the story of a remarkable mother in a poor area of Chicago and how she was raising her son, who then was about twelve or thirteen. She had chosen to commit all her energies to saving her boy from the lure of the streets. She kept strict tabs on him, insisting he call from wherever he was. She made sure he kept up with his schoolwork. She made herself available to him. Finally, she was making plans to send him away to a college-prep military school in the far suburbs. Her son, in turn, was bright, well-mannered, and articulate.

It's possible the mother had advantages I was unaware of—strong and caring parents, some education, things that give a person a leg up in life. It would be simplistic to say that all we have to do is choose what we want, then go for it. Some of us are hampered by poverty, disability, or a dysfunctional background. The only attitudes we've ever seen modeled are negative and defeatist.

Yet we've all seen people overcome even those toxic legacies—and we've also seen people who, like the Prodigal Son, squandered a rich inheritance. Somewhere along the line, a choice was made, or a series of choices.

We may not be able to remove every roadblock from our lives. We can, however, choose to shake that victim mentality—and with God's help get unstuck from the clutter.

We won't stay unstuck, though, until we recognize and admit our weakness in the face of sin and how it can worm its way into our everyday lives.

Getting Specific About Sin

Sin. Not a subject most of us care to dwell on, unless it's sin in the abstract. It's easy enough to quote Romans 3:23—

oh, yeah, we've all sinned; it's the human condition. It's quite another challenge to stand in God's searchlight and confess, "Lord, I sinned when I failed to comfort a friend when she needed me. I sinned when I said some harsh things to my mother. I sinned when I harbored vindictive feelings toward the person who hurt me so much instead of working toward forgiveness."

Recently my husband and I went to hear a friend of ours preach his second sermon at his new church. Our friend, Greg, did a bold thing: He preached on sin. More often new pastors preach affirming messages on how happy they are to be there, and it's a new beginning, and then everybody leaves feeling good. Greg, an upbeat sort of guy who came out of youth ministry, could have pulled that off easily. Instead he spoke of the reality of sin—not just abstract, theological fallenness, which is easy to dismiss, or the sins of all those bad, worldly people outside the church, but specific sins such as ignoring the needs of the poor or letting others down.

Every now and then it's good medicine to hear a message like that. Not because we need to be scolded, but because it reminds us that sins have names, that, as Oswald Chambers notes, "Whenever you talk about sin, it must be 'my' sin. So long as you speak of 'sins' you evade Jesus Christ for yourself."[1]

Confessing our sin does not mean we wallow in some sort of medieval self-abasement. Confessing our particular, specific, real-life sins opens up the secret recesses of our soul to the vigorous and sometimes painful scrubbing of God's grace. It helps us understand why things don't change and why things *can't* change until we admit an absolute and radical dependence on God and His saving work. It helps us understand why, as my pastor, John Benson, said, "Doing the wrong thing seems so easy, like paddling downstream with the current. Doing the right thing is like paddling upstream against the current."

How do we navigate the current? We don't, because we

can't. Jay Phelan, editor of *The Covenant Companion*, observes that *"Thinking* right or *being* right has never gotten anybody right. Turning in desolation and hope to Jesus *has.* Staying in the loving and purging presence of Jesus *has."*[2]

We have a Nativity scene we set out when Advent begins. It's an olivewood set of figures carved in the Holy Land, a gift of a women's group I used to lead when we were in the pastorate. Each night we move Mary and Joseph ("and the donkey," my daughter reminded me) a little farther along to where the Infant lies in the manger. Across the corner table, over the bookshelves, onto the windowsill, and finally, on Christmas Day, to the hutch where the stable is set up. It's our family's way of journeying toward the Birth (remember what I said about my daughter being a hands-on learner), of sharing a joyful expectancy.

The figure of the Christ Child is somewhat roughly carved. The baby is not beautiful; in fact, it has a rather strange, squinched-up face. But I love that crèche. It's a hands-on reminder of, in the words of Pope John Paul II, "God's supreme humility." The Word become flesh. Flesh like ours, yet not like ours. Flesh that, in our behalf, felt the pain of spikelike nails.

I don't know about you, but when I reflect on that incredible gift . . . I want to give something back, acknowledge it in some way. I *want* to become more worthy of that loving Presence.

When I reflect on that incredible gift . . . I want to give something back, acknowledge it in some way.

When I was about sixteen my mother stayed up half the night typing my high-school term paper. I had known about it for weeks, of course. But I let it go until days before it was due. My mother might have alluded to that fact—but she also knew that the paper constituted something like half my semester grade. So well into the night I slept and woke, slept and woke to the sound of the manual typewriter pecking away in the next room.

In my adolescent self-centeredness, I did not think much about my mother's sacrifice at the time. I was just relieved she bailed me out (again). Now, as a mother myself, I am awed by her mercy—on that and other occasions. Because she has, time and again, shown her unconditional love to me, I am moved to respond to that love, to *do* something about it. And it isn't burdensome. It's a joy.

So it is with our relationship to God. Our obedience comes not from fear, but from love.

The Blessing of Limits

God is not a capricious parent. His limits on us really are, as we're fond of telling our own kids, "for our own good." One of the lessons I've been trying to teach Amanda is that the limits her dad and I set for her come out of our love for her and our hope that she grow as Christ would have her to do. As I spent untold hours working as a cashier at our school book fair, I was frankly appalled to see how popular some of the horror books are with children Amanda's age, including kids I'm sure come from Christian homes. Once Amanda brought one of these titles home from the public library. (I'm not going to mention the name, because I don't want to give them free publicity, but you who have middle-reader children probably know the series I mean.) It was about a boy who became invisible. Well, that didn't seem too harmful; what kid hasn't wanted to be invisible? Rather than censor it out of hand—and encourage the forbidden-fruit syndrome—I said I would read the book aloud to her (it was short).

Yuck. As I finished reading I wished I had skimmed the pages first. I felt unsettled, brushed with something *wrong*.

There was no redeeming good-over-evil triumph. The tone was nasty, nihilistic, horror for horror's sake.

I explained to Amanda that books like this are not what God wants for her. I reminded her of the *McGee and Me!* video we had watched, the one where Nicholas sneaks out to see a gory movie and gets in trouble. And I said, "We're not reading any more of these. I don't care what the other kids do; I don't want this stuff around."

At first she protested ("It's only a book, Mom!"). But I noticed she didn't ask to buy any of the titles at the book fair, nor has she brought any home from the library. I noticed she told a friend, with some pride, "I'm not allowed to read those stories." Limits imposed out of love.

I want to tack on a disclaimer that the limits-equals-love argument does not always work so perfectly with her! But we're trying, and, as she gets older, I think the message is starting to get through. Likewise, as we grow in Christian maturity (and see the wreckage that can come from living *outside* God's limits), living inside God's restrictions can feel like a pretty safe place to be.

Too often I have to consciously think, "Okay, now it's time to stop procrastinating and get down to work." It takes effort, whereas laziness comes naturally and seems more fun.

But again, as with Amanda, we don't always get the message. As much as we love God and want to serve Him, we're still paddling against the current of our own willfulness. Too often I have to consciously think, *Okay, now it's time to stop procrastinating and get down to work.* It takes *effort*, whereas laziness comes naturally and seems more fun. But the point is not that we "solve" the problem once and for all, but that we're moving in the right direction. That we know we're weak and fearful, but our longing to know God is more powerful than the fear that keeps us mired in our fallenness. We would, in the midst of the world's demands, see Jesus. We can—even as we're bending over to retrieve dropped balls. We might even see Him on His knees, helping us pick up those balls. And I have a feeling there might be an amused little smile on His face.

Notes

1. *Oswald Chambers: The Best of All His Books*, edited by Harry Verploegh (Thomas Nelson, 1989), p. 299.
2. John E. Phelan, Jr., "Markings" column, *The Covenant Companion* (September 1995), p. 5.

8

On Clothespins and Katydids and February Mondays; or, Why I'm *Not* Going to Disney World

SEE GOD IN THE EVERYDAY. Yes, of course we do. Don't we?

It sounds so easy, doesn't it? Almost trite. See God in the face of a child, in an opening flower, Orion striding across the winter sky. Look for God's blessings in the small gifts; be alert to those times, as when God himself told Elijah, "The Lord is passing by."

Sometimes, though, seeing God in the everyday can seem like something we have to . . . work at. I once heard someone joke, "When I get up in the morning, my attitude is, When morning gilds the skies, my heart awaking cries, 'Oh no, another day.' "

You know you're blessed. Your kids are healthy, you are ambulatory most days, you have a roof over your head. But instead you focus on what you don't have, thinking, *I still need to lose weight. We have no money and no hope of it ever getting better. We still have that ugly orange-and-green '60s bathroom wallpaper we inherited when we moved into this house.* My idea of a blessing is buy-one-get-one-free day at the market.

Okay, I sound cynical, but you know what I mean. We're

bombarded with these messages—"Stop and smell the roses!" And *sometimes* we can affirm that. We know how to stop and smell the roses. Other times . . . we just know they'll have thorns. Besides, we'd enjoy them better if we were viewing them from the front porch of our rambling summer cottage, preferably while the gardener pruned them artistically.

Many of us have seen or read the play *Our Town*, by Thornton Wilder, about ordinary people in a turn-of-the-century New England hamlet. Probably the most famous passage is where Emily, a young woman who dies in childbirth, reflects from the afterlife about the preciousness of life and how few people really see, really savor, really *live* that life while on earth.

An incident at our house a few months back got me thinking about this. One afternoon my husband was out playing basketball in the driveway with our daughter. After she had given him a sound thrashing in a game of Horse, he came in and said, "You know, when I was a kid I always dreamed of this—being married, having a child to do sports with. Girl or boy, it didn't matter. It's important to recognize when your dreams come true."

A dream, fulfilled by throwing a ball through a second-hand net on a chilly day. Just everyday, unexciting stuff—and, I believe, the stuff of God. But oh, so easy to ignore.

Often, looking for God in the everyday feels like searching through that aforementioned junk drawer for your engagement ring. We call out, "God, I know you're in here . . . somewhere . . ." and we don't hear His voice quietly saying, "I'm right here in front of you. I'm in this day, in this place, in everything that happens."

Quiet Joy—or a Dull Life?

Why is it so hard to know quiet joy—or even just a mild satisfaction? You can blame it, in part, on the world we live in. The world doesn't value the father shooting hoops with his kid; it values the NBA multizillionaire hitting the three-pointer to win the championship. The world doesn't value sitting around on the front porch; it values trips to Disney World. The world doesn't value sacrifice; it values the quest for "fulfillment."

The world doesn't notice things. Are the clouds sailing overhead cirrus or cumulus? What phase is the moon in? Ever see the way earthworms crawl out after a heavy spring rain? Hear the katydids in August? "Can't say as I have," responds the world. "Been glued to my new Windows '95." (Nothing makes me feel older and more out of it than watching the young folks getting excited about some new technological gizmo. Now I know how my parents felt when the Beatles were on *The Ed Sullivan Show*.)

There's one particularly odious radio commercial that's been running in our area. The announcer asks a supposed Everyman, "What are *you* doing tonight?" and the boring guy responds apologetically, "Working the crossword puzzle and changing the litter box." And the announcer exclaims, "Well, come to the riverboat casino!" Forget your dull life, you slug. Go waste hundreds of dollars at the slot machines. And don't even come up on the deck for air.

And that, much of the time, is the world we all live in, including Christians. I suppose it would be possible to wall oneself off and only listen to Christian radio and watch Christian TV and read Christian books and get a job in Christian work and send one's kids to Christian schools and look for Christian merchants to patronize. Some people come close to that sort of cloistering, and I can see why. But we still have to reckon with neighbors and relatives. I haven't yet discovered a "Christian" way to shop for a new car or get on an airplane or stand in the checkout line at the grocery store. (Maybe with your eyes closed so you don't have to look at those scandal sheets.)

There's so much in the everyday that's so *ungodly*. Disappointment, conflict, wrong relationships. And the wrongness isn't just out there in the pagans. It's in us. I was arguing about this with a nonevangelical Christian recently. Quoting a figure that claimed that 70 percent of men have been unfaithful to their wives, she said, "And the church is no different." I hotly took issue with that statement. "At least we *try*," I said. Then I read about a prominent Christian woman who confessed to having affairs while she was married. I thought I was used to scandal, but this one really appalled me, maybe because it was a woman, and I believe that, as much as men are called to love and serve their wives—to be the "promise keepers"—we women are called to be the "relationship keepers," to tend those home fires and keep them glowing. It just seemed like such a failure of integrity, and it made me wonder if we *are* so different.

I haven't yet discovered a "Christian" way to shop for a new car or get on an airplane or stand in the checkout line at the grocery store.

So it's easy to become corroded by cynicism, to never lift our eyes unto the hills but keep looking down at the dust as we plod along. I vividly recall what a woman of my acquaintance, a longtime Christian, once said in a group. "I know I'm saved," she reflected, "but where's the joy?" Being a Christian didn't seem to be making any difference in her day-to-day *reality*. Shouldn't she feel happier, more content, more hopeful?

Worship Out of Work

One way to seek God in the everyday is to look toward people who seem to be getting it right. When I'm tempted to become discouraged about God's people, I think of Pat and Patty. I've changed a lot of details in this sketch because they'd be embarrassed at being held up as godly examples. You may know people like them, too. Pat and Patty don't have a lot of money. Pat owns a landscaping business, and Patty works part time as a teacher's aide. They drive used vans and live in an unremarkable ranch house, which Pat has fixed up over the years. Patty can squeeze the American dollar until George Washington cries for mercy, but she never complains. They're the first to offer help when something needs doing around the church; Patty will babysit your kids in a pinch; Pat will do odd jobs around your house and not even mention payment. Like most suburban couples with kids, Pat and Patty are busy. Their kids are busy, too. But when you talk to them, they always seem as if they have all the time in the world. Pat tells funny stories; Patty will listen to you and laugh at your jokes. There's something unhurried and innately gracious about them—something almost old-fashioned. They seem content and they live fairly simply, but they don't make a big, guilt-inducing deal out of being content and living simply, if you know what I mean. They don't take themselves very seriously.

What's their secret?

They seem to have a good marriage . . . but so do a lot of people. They have good values . . . but so do a lot of people. After puzzling on this for a while, I've come to the conclusion that Pat and Patty seem to be living with a certain sanity and balance. They aren't driven by the crazy push to achieve and attain. Their doing *for* God comes out of their being *with* God.

Others among us look as if we're the most dedicated of the Lord's servants, but inside we're like a dry hole in West Texas, sucked of all its oil. In fact, I think that's more common than people realize. We're really adept at talking the talk, smiling the smile, appearing so spiritual. We can even lie to ourselves . . . for a while. But we can't lie to God.

Another woman in my church (I have a great church;

come and visit us sometime) shared an insight I thought profound in its truth. A lifelong believer, she had been struggling with some of those same feelings of dryness, of doing but not really being—the familiar Martha syndrome. She finally concluded that her *work* had to come out of her *worship*. Not the other way around.

To see God in the everyday doesn't so much mean forcing yourself in some mechanical way to notice things—that's that work emphasis again—as it does creating the conditions for receptivity, fostering a refreshed alertness. Evelyn Christenson observes that a simple good night's sleep clears the clutter out of her mind. "Often," she says, "I lie in bed, completely open to the Lord."

Your Own Secret Places

Across from the office building of my former employer, there used to be an empty lot. Well, most people thought it was an empty lot. I loved it. I would go walking in it on my lunch hour and discover wild strawberries, watch goldfinches, jump out of the way of flying grasshoppers, hide among the thickety trees and bushes, think about the farm that once occupied the land. No one else ever came in there; it was "my" place.

One day I saw a "Lot for Sale: Build to Suit" sign on my place. I thought about sneaking out in the dead of night to take the sign down, like one of those environmental activists you hear about. But of course I didn't. I resigned myself to the inevitable and watched the trees get bulldozed, the finches get routed out of their homes, the strawberries vanish. In time an attractive brick office building on a manicured lawn dotted with fake hills went up. I could console myself that at least it wasn't a strip mall. But it was sterile . . . *predictable*. Nothing to discover. I missed my wild, brushy, uncontrolled place.

We need to allow ourselves those little undiscovered places of the soul, those times when we don't have to be anywhere or do anything, moments when we can say to ourselves, "Let's see, what shall I do now? I could polish the silver, or write a letter, or make some soup, or go for a walk . . ."

And I could be with God. To fold ourselves in quiet, actively waiting on Him, enjoying His world. I've learned that I absolutely have to do physical stuff to freshen my spirit. At times I think I might be really content if we lived on a *Charlotte's Web* sort of fantasy farm, and I spent most of my time gardening and cooking and maybe taking care of a couple of friendly pigs. I wouldn't worry about professional stuff; I'd bake pies for the county fair and have a peach orchard and a nice-smelling barn. (Of course, since neither my husband nor I know how to do much of this, Pat and Patty would have to move in with us, because Pat was raised on a farm and knows how to do everything.)

My dad bequeathed a lot of things to me, among them the temperament of an Irish artist, which means that sometimes the world can look like a very dark place. But he also passed on a favorite saying: "Work, don't think." He knew that when he was idle, he would start to brood. I do the same. So when I find myself lapsing into melancholy, I dig or sweep or scrub. Hanging laundry is great—I highly recommend it. (Unless you live in one of those hoity-toity neighborhoods that bans clotheslines.) For me, hands-on work seems to, literally and figuratively, clear out the cobwebs.

Pondering time. Puttering time. Are you allowing yourself enough of these little open corners?

Pondering time. Puttering time. Are you allowing yourself enough of these little open corners? ("What do you mean, 'allow'?" I can hear you arguing. "Like I have a choice. Do you know how crazy my life is these days?")

To which I respond, like the sister always ready to give frank advice: Do you know that you could *de*-craze your life if you found a way to build in these times? Are you very certain there isn't an element of pride in being so busy?

The Risks of Routine

There is, however, another side to this, one we don't always hear about. Sometimes that "oh no, another day" feeling descends not because we're overloaded, but because we're *underloaded*. We need downtime, but we also need stimulation and variety. A couple of years ago I was on a business trip out East, and I spent some time with my kid sister and her husband in New York City. It was a Saturday night, and we were driving through midtown on our way to eat in Greenwich Village, and I kept pointing and exclaiming: "Look! The Empire State Building! Look! That's the Public Library, just like in movies I've seen!" The car had a sunroof and I kept threatening to stand up in it, like some footloose teenager. My sister looked at me, grinning, and said, "You really need stimulation."

Well, she was right, and stimulation isn't always easy to come by when you work at home. Of course, it isn't that easy when you're in the same office day after day, either. I'm not saying we always have to go seeking entertainment. But *too much* "everyday" can keep us from seeing God. Too much routine can dull our senses and spirits to His activity among us. Minds need workouts as much as muscles do. To do something different—visit another church on a Sunday, discover an author new to us, go on an architectural tour of old homes, play hooky for a day and take the train downtown— these things stretch us. In a small way, they're little baby steps of risk that pull us out of the familiar.

And I believe God honors that, the way He honored all those women and men in the Bible who chose to step out.

In fact, I think it pleases God when we make an effort to grow in Him by reaching a bit, not coasting on the known and comfortable.

Curiosity, too, is a wonderful thing. Our kids are forever asking "why" questions. Do we? Just now as I was looking out the window, I saw a little squirrel hopping around our lawn. Okay, all squirrels are little, but this guy was really small, because he had only a stump of a tail. It set me wondering: How does he get around? Can he climb, jump, balance on wires like his more endowed brothers? Is this rare? Do other squirrels notice that he's different? (Hey, who needs Manhattan when we can watch squirrels!) Whimsical wondering about how and why God's world works takes us out of ourselves and deepens our desire to know Him and receive even His smallest gifts.

Whimsical wondering about how and why God's world works takes us out of ourselves and deepens our desire to know Him and receive even His smallest gifts.

Think about it: How often do life's peak moments come to us? Once a year I get to stand at the edge of the continent, watching the ocean waves roll in, feeling shivery and dramatic and wondering if my hair is rippling artistically in the breeze. The rest of the time I'm here in the Midwest, looking out my window at overgrown bushes and garage roofs and wondering if I have coffee breath. But because God has put me here, I know He wants me to make the most of this life— to see His light shining through the ordinary. And it occurs to me that this light may even be a little glimmer of what we shall find someday in eternity, that God loves us so much He wants to give us a little preview. Rated for general audiences.

9

Was That the Lord, or My Own Wishful Thinking?

YOU'RE SITTING IN PRAYER, agonizing over a decision. "Tell me, Lord!" you implore. "Guide me!" You know you probably aren't going to hear some clear call, but you want to do as God leads. You seek confirmation from friends and trusted fellow believers. You search the Scriptures. Finally, a plan forms in your mind. This, you think, is what God is leading you toward.

You think. But in the back of your mind, there's a tiny voice of doubt: Is it *really* God, or is it me?

This doubt, this second-guessing, this blundering along in the half-light, feels like clutter to us, like unnecessary baggage burdening us in our Christian walk. Mother Teresa has no such doubts. Catherine Marshall probably didn't either. The soloist who sang at the Sunday evening service sure didn't seem to wonder, not with that fixed smile.

If you listen to some people, you get the idea that they are saints so effortlessly in tune with God's will (according to them, at least) that every morning they boot up their computers and God has e-mailed them a personal blueprint for their day, complete with cute little icons to show

"Here's what to do about your work"—"Here's the path to take with your kids"—"This is the answer for your money problems."

These people say things like, "I turned to the Bible and there was the answer"—the close-your-eyes-and-point strategy. I close my eyes and point, and the answer I get is that God wants me to go out and slay the Amalekites.

These people claim immediate guidance in response to prayer. Sometimes that happens to me, but more often not. More often God seems like my mother. When I was a kid and would want something—"Mom, can I get a pony? We could keep it in the yard." She'd say, "We'll see." God seems to be saying that to me: "We'll see." Don't call me, I'll call you. I often fail to see the connection between my requests and what God gives me.

God's Plans and Our Choices

Lately, too, I've been looking at situations from the back end—how they came out—and wondering about this business of guidance. It's a little like a *Nightline* segment I saw once, a year-end review in which several pundits made predictions for the coming year and looked back on their forecasts for the year ending. Some of the predictions had been accurate, others not.

It's easy to say we feel "led" by the Lord toward something—but then what actually happens? I know people who were very sure that God was guiding them to certain marriage partners—then the unions dissolved amid charges of abuse, infidelity, and just plain falling out of love. I know people who felt strongly led to pursue a ministry for which they were uniquely gifted, but then family needs forced them to put their dreams on hold. I know people who prayed over launching a new business and secured the necessary capital and handled everything according to biblical principles, but the business still failed. I know churches that felt God was directing them to start a "daughter congregation" in a growing community, but the church plant withered before it bore any fruit.

These are the stories of failure you *don't* hear about—but they happen all the time. We don't like to hear about them because they seem to go against everything we've been told. If God is calling you to a certain path, doesn't He remove all obstacles? Doesn't Proverbs tell us that if we commit our plans to the Lord, we will succeed (3:6)? Did these people not have enough faith?

Remember my talking about the difficult time when I sought counsel from my pastor? Some of my struggle involved my sense of call. I had about come to the conclusion that I was not called to a ministry of writing and speaking, as I had thought, because the Lord did not seem to be blessing the work materially, and wasn't that a sign He wanted me to go do something else? I mean, how long do I have to wait on this, God? It's been two years and I want something really big to happen.

I can laugh about it now (and I'm sure I probably gave God a chuckle or two). It wasn't funny at the time, though. I truly wondered where I fit, what He wanted of me. I was trying to surrender my will to His. If He would just tell me what to do, I wouldn't be like Jonah. I'd go.

Well, okay, so what happened? Eventually I got sick of myself and my constant whining, and I have a sneaking suspicion those very feelings may have been a clue that God was getting sick of me too—the way we can love a friend dearly but secretly feel impatient with her endless problems and wish she would grow up and take her life in her hands. I had a sense that God was saying, "Look: Take the long view. Look at the big picture. Admittedly, for you that's much smaller than My big picture—but give it a shot. Use your head. Meanwhile . . . trust Me."

God wanted *me* to take responsibility, to understand that a call is not a blueprint. It's more of a rough outline that we're supposed to fill in. He's given us the freedom to work out the details, to make the choices that will get us from point A to point B.

He's also given us the freedom to fail, you know. He gives us the freedom to make bad judgments. Why He sometimes chooses to let us make really disastrous mistakes, such as marrying the wrong person or losing everything in a poor business investment, we don't know. It may have something to do with His desire to teach us; it may have a great deal to do with our own human arrogance and fallenness. It may also have something to do with His desire for us to grow, rather than His stepping in and taking over.

God wanted me to take responsibility, to understand that a call is not a blueprint.

But there are some clues as to God's broad outline. If He gives us a gift, chances are He intends for us to use it in some way. (See Ephesians 4:12.) If we are growing in Him, are spending time in prayer, worship, and the Word, and are connected to wise and godly believers, we are at least giving ourselves a fighting chance to make the right choices. God does not wish us to harm another. When we do fail, He does not wish us to look back in hand-wringing, but to consider what good may come out of the bad. And He wants us to look toward the character of Christ as our model.

Good Feelings Aren't a Given

Notice I haven't said anything about having that "sense of peace" everyone talks about. It's easy to confuse a sense of peace with a good mood. To be honest, I don't always feel wonderful about my work. I can feel lonely and uninspired and dream about that farm I mentioned earlier. I can feel a sense of peace while I'm baking bread, but that doesn't mean I'm called to be a pastry chef like my friend Sharon. Think of the great pioneer missionaries like William Carey and Adoniram Judson: My guess is their sense of guidance had very little to do with *feeling* that their ministries were really being blessed and the harvest of souls was increasing every day. Wives and children succumbed to illnesses; sometimes they were in physical danger. But they were obedient to their sense of call.

This has been perhaps the hardest lesson for me to learn, that I won't always *feel* great about what I'm doing— but I have to do it anyway. Because *over time* I've learned that I'll probably always ride the good-day/bad-day roller coaster, but that doesn't mean I have to take up residence there. Over time I've devoted a considerable amount of prayer to this question. Over time I've received enough confirmation to believe that, yes, I am called to what I'm doing, and emulating the character of Christ means that I am to be faithful and obedient, as He is faithful and obedient.

Trusting God for the big stuff and worrying less about the niggling little points of guidance actually freed me to start seeing my problems more clearly—and seeing God more clearly. Looking back, I realize now that throughout that hard time I was *with God* in a powerful, intimate, beyond-words sort of way. I did not always love God during that period; often, I was impatient with Him, baffled by His ways. God, however, was faithful. Not "faithful" in the *quid pro quo* sense we sometimes understand that word: If we're good Christians, He'll make life go right for us. But faithful in the sense that He was giving me himself and His presence, that He was teaching me to draw nearer to Him. Faithful in the sense that, even when I was a self-involved mess, He loved me and was infinitely patient with me.

The experience brought home Paul's words to Timothy:

"But for that very reason I was shown mercy so that in me, the worst of sinners, Christ Jesus might display his unlimited patience as an example for those who would believe on him and receive eternal life" (1 Timothy 1:16).

Thy Will Be Done

Part of the reason we can struggle so much with seeking God's will for our lives is that we boldface the "our" and not the "God." God *is* concerned about the details of our lives, as I've said repeatedly in this book. He *does* work in and through these things. But there's a powerful and subtle temptation to become so preoccupied with our plans we lose sight of the fact that God, being God, has no obligation to provide us with ready-made responses to those plans or to submit an alternative plan of His own.

" 'For my thoughts are not your thoughts, neither are your ways my ways,' declares the Lord" (Isaiah 55:8). But note that this is not some arrogant brushing off of our gnatlike concerns. In verses 2–3, God invites us: "Listen, listen to me, and eat what is good, and your soul will delight in the richest of fare. Give ear and come to me; hear me, that your soul may live." Later He promises that the word that goes out from His mouth "will not return to me empty, but will accomplish what I desire and achieve the purpose for which I sent it" (v. 11). What *He* desires— through us.

Our Sunday school class at church was discussing these guidance questions a while back. One woman kept asking, with honesty and simplicity, "But how do you *know*? How can you know for sure that you're doing what God wants?"

I'm not sure that we ever do know, completely. We see through a mirror dimly; we know in part. Where the outline has blank spaces, we fill in with trust. It is by *not knowing*, but trying to understand a little bit, that we move toward God.

And by having no illusions about the fallen world we temporarily inhabit. In the *Wrestling With Angels* video series, Philip Yancey quotes a man of his acquaintance, someone who had suffered terribly, as saying, "You can't confuse God with life." God instituted marriage, but in a fallen world—in life—spouses do terrible things to each other. God loves His church, but in our fallen world, those who need her most are sometimes stubbornly resistant to her invitation. God calls on us to trust, but Satan is right there whispering words of discouragement.

It is by not knowing, but trying to understand a little bit, that we move toward God.

Remember the writing school I mentioned, the one I did some teaching for? Even though I wanted out of the relationship, I was still concerned when it ended. There was a moment of panic: What will I do to fill in the lost income? But very quickly I prayed—aloud—"Lord, protect me from discouragement." Satan knows our weak areas and will always exploit them. Mine is the temptation to get discouraged, to ride that roller coaster. I'm finding that every day I need to call upon the Lord to cover that chink in my armor.

Which brings us back to one of my main themes in this book, that God leads us toward Him by giving us responsibility. I've heard it said more than once that "God can't move a stone." Of course He can (I'm sure He shuffled a few mountain ranges around in the process of Creation), but the point is that He expects us to take *some* action. I have a friend whose husband went from job to job, but nothing quite fit. They prayed continually for God to show them the way, but door after door seemed to slam shut in their faces.

Meanwhile, they had no money, they had a growing family, and they were running out of doors. Finally they decided to act: They put their house on the market. My friend admitted to me she had no idea exactly where they were going to go, but they had to set a process in motion, break the logjam of doing nothing.

God leads us toward Himself by giving us responsibility.

A few months later an opportunity came up in another state, and they took it. It wasn't a great now-our-troubles-are-over solution, but they were trusting God for the _process_. According to my friend, the experience has strengthened their marriage and their walk with the Lord, but they've still had some tough times since they moved. They continue to wait on God. And this, perhaps, may be the very hardest part of the Christian life.

Waiting

There are so many areas where we can feel as if we're going nowhere, spinning our wheels. "Waiting on the Lord" is one of those things that sounds really spiritual and sacrificial, but sometimes, when you actually have to do it, it's about as much fun as hanging out at an airport gate for a plane that never arrives, and all there is to read are back issues of _USA Today_, and all there is to eat are the breath mints in our pocket, and the TV is tuned to the golf channel.

I know of so many people who have been waiting—and searching—for years. Every path they've taken seems to lead to a dead end. Some of these people have advanced degrees in Bible and theology; others ingested Christianity with their mother's milk. They know the passages, the promises, the prayers. But they struggle with cynicism: Does God *really* guide, really care? Lord, how long wilt Thou hide Thy face from me?

I wish I had some easy response to such pain. I don't. I don't get it. I think it's really unfair that one man I know can't seem to find the work he wants, while another has so much but doesn't seem to be grateful. It bothers me a lot that a woman who has served God all her life has suffered one disappointment after another. It makes me angry—not with God, but with life.

I don't have a response, but the Bible does. This is what the writer of Hebrews meant when he or she spoke of being "certain of what we do not see" (11:1).

As a friend of mine wisely observed, "A lot of Scripture is really one foot, other foot." The Bible, she noted, compresses time so we think of things happening quickly—but, for example, it must have taken Noah a very long time to build the ark. "And nowhere," my friend added, "does it say he was a skilled carpenter!" Four hundred fifty feet is *long*. (For comparison, a football field is 300 feet. Most ballparks aren't more than 415 feet or so at their deepest point.) He and his sons had to go cut down the cypress logs, trim them, somehow drag them to the building site, saw them into boards, nail them together . . . I get worn out just thinking about it.

Persevering

Peter sees fit to include "perseverance" in his list of qualities that will make the believer effective and productive in her knowledge of Christ (2 Peter 1:6). Goodness, knowledge, godliness, kindness, love, are sort of the "glamor" attributes—visible, admirable. Hardly anyone lauds somebody by saying, "And he's so persevering!" But plain old perseverance is what enables us to live out these other traits day in, day out. Hanging in there. Sticking to it. Building an ark or a family or a friendship or a faith. Persevering because, like Moses, we "[see] him who is invisible" (Hebrews 11:27).

And maybe we're not persevering *toward* something—ever thought of that? Maybe we hang in because we're *already* where God wants us to be, and our faithfulness is a response to His faithfulness. When we think of guidance, of what we wish God would do in our lives, we tend to fixate on the future, on something we don't have. We look at the hole instead of the doughnut (or bagel, if you want to be healthy about it).

That was something else I discovered when I was wondering about my call. When it seemed as if my life was pretty much staying in the same place, it occurred to me that maybe that in itself was a "sign." God wasn't opening a door; He wasn't closing a door: He was telling me, in effect, "You're already in the room."

God wasn't opening a door; He wasn't closing a door: He was telling me, in effect, "You're already in the room."

Has it ever happened to you that you thought a door was closed tight, and you shoved on it and practically fell through because the door wasn't really shut tight? God's guidance to us can be like that: The door was open all the time, and all we had to do was consider that possibility and step across the threshold. Or maybe we have to get our tools and keep fiddling. Or it could be that we have to ask ourselves if we're even in the right building!

God alone knows the plans He has for us (Jeremiah 29:11), and, always, they are better than we think those plans should be. Meanwhile, whether we're twiddling around waiting for the door to open or have already stumbled through, we can, as David counsels, "delight in the Lord." Delight in Him for who He is and how He has shown himself to us in so many ways. Sweep away the clutter of fixating on the future and agonizing over every jot and tittle of interpreting His will. It's simpler than we think: God loves us and wants the best for us. Maybe that best is here now; maybe it's still to come; maybe even both. In the meantime, we can rest in Him who saw that it was good.

10

Christ and Connectedness

WELL, HERE WE ALL ARE, feeling, a lot of the time, more like the walking wounded than God's mighty army. Here we are in our sin and busyness and struggle and wrong thinking; here we are trying to make sense of the clutter and get rid of those spiritual broken crayons and old newspapers and meaningless screws. Here we all are, hoping that someday, somewhere, the emotional drawers of our lives will be organized and clean. And here we all are, thinking that *no one else* feels the same way, that no one else has ever wondered whether God loves her, and that nobody except us has a spiritual life that looks better on the outside than it is on the inside.

Recently I sat in a group of thirty women at my church. We're trying to launch a viable women's ministry after the old women's group sputtered and finally expired. As we sat there sharing ideas for what such a ministry would look like, I could *feel* a current of need rippling through the room. Stories bursting to be told. Struggles straining to be shared. Some of us said, "Let's have fun!" Others wanted a book group, crafts, service projects, exercising. Still others just wanted to do coffee and talk. But, to a woman, we all wanted to connect, to know and be known. I thought, not for the first time, *This is where God moves. This is who He uses. We are His hands . . . and when we join those hands, great things can happen.*

We are His hands . . . and when we join those hands, great things can happen.

"I Have What You Have!"

Paul's words in Philippians on being "content in all things" are familiar to all of us, even, sometimes, guilt inducing. But it's significant to me that he goes on to write, "Yet it was good of you to share in my troubles" (4:14). *Christ* is sufficient, but *Paul* is insufficient. He can't go on pridefully independent. He needs others to help in his ministry, to pray for him, to bounce his ideas off of, to give him lodging. Charles Swindoll even speculates that Luke may have traveled with Paul to serve as his personal physician. Paul needs all those people who, in small ways, reflect the light of Christ. And so do we. At least as important, we need to *be* those people.

As we look at these questions of seeking God's light in the dim everyday, of starting where we are and shedding the clutter that keeps us from fully grasping His hand, the temptation is to feel alone on the journey, to lament, "Nobody knows the trouble I've seen." Oh, woe is me, a solitary pilgrim on life's road. There can be almost a prideful sense that we're so sensitive and so complex that no one else could possibly have the same struggles we do. "You're alone" is one of Satan's most devastating lies.

Wasn't it Tolstoy who said that each unhappy family is

unhappy in its own way? (I'm no better at remembering famous quotes than I am at remembering jokes. But for the sake of argument, let's assume he said that.) Anyway, I'm not sure I agree. When you really start talking with other people, really start to share deeply, you realize that you aren't unique in your problems and anxieties. That in itself can be wondrously healing—you mean I'm *not* crazy after all? I'm not a horrible mother? I'm not a dangerous heretic?

"You're alone" is one of Satan's most devastating lies.

Remember the summer of 1995? It was horribly hot in a lot of places, including the Midwest. I was sick of air conditioning, sick of humidity but no rain, sick of feeling enervated and almost hopeless. I was feeling depressed, but it was a different sort of depression than that which had led me to seek counseling from my pastor. Near the merciful end of that summer, a friend called. She's moved out of the area, so we don't see each other as often as we would like, but she's very special to me. As we chatted, she mentioned that she thought she suffered from summer depression, which always abated when the weather cooled off. A light went on in my head. "Wait a minute!" I crowed. "I think I have that too!"

"You do?" she responded with surprise.

"Yeah. Around late May or June, I start getting crabby and negative. I'm realizing now that it's been a pattern with me for the last several years, and I usually pull out of it when fall comes."

We talked some more about why this is, about the nuances of the creative personality (she's a musician), about the underestimated impact of weather on the soul, and how we both get our creative juices going once the weather gets cold. When I hung up I felt . . . cured. It was still hot and I was still depressed, but now I knew why. It would end. It was better, and cheaper, than going to a therapist.

God used my friend to break through the summer blahs, to help me understand a little more about myself. *I have what you have. You're not alone.* Now, when summer comes around again, I'll be alert to those signs and try not to be such a victim of my glands or whatever it is that makes a person hypersensitive to weather.

Of course, it isn't always that easy. Merely sharing a problem does not guarantee solving that problem. But it's where we have to start—speaking and listening, praying and encouraging, giving and receiving.

The Power of Presence

Have you ever wished you could fix people's problems? Maybe it's the mom in a lot of us, wanting to put a bandage on the boo-boo and make it go away. I'm a pretty good idea person, too. I can become frustrated as I watch a friend struggle with money. I want to suggest to her ideas for starting a new home business. I'll even be willing to do some networking for her, pass on her name to some people I know who are in a position to use her talents. Ask Betsey; she'll solve your problems. (Other people's problems are always easier to solve than one's own. . . .) I have friends who are struggling with new babies, friends seeking God's will in their lives, friends who want to work but aren't sure what they should do, friends with teenagers . . .

I don't think we're a particularly needy lot. I think we're typical. But I want to fix things for my friends. I find it hard to stand by and watch them struggle. Sometimes it doesn't seem like "enough" to listen, to pray, to support.

My pastor once preached on the power of prayer. He dryly observed that, in many churches, we use the term "prayer warriors" to designate those who can't do anything else. They can't get out to meetings, don't have enough energy for the youth group, can't carry a tune for the choir, and can't see well enough to read Scripture in worship. So they can stay at home and do the passive work of praying, while the "real" work of the church gets done by those younger and stronger.

It's the same with friendship. We may think we're incapable of being a worthwhile friend, a friend who can really make a difference in someone else's life. We can wonder, *What do I have to offer?*

We can offer ourselves, our presence, our love.

We never know whom we may be touching and what consequences it may have. I've been thinking about this recently, the impact we have on others, sometimes unbeknownst to us. I want to tell you about a woman who just went to be with the Lord, because her story needs to be told. Her name is Bonnie Rice. She wasn't famous or wealthy. She died of cancer at the age of sixty-five—too young, too young. My husband, daughter, and I went to her wake, and as we entered I whispered to Fritz, "Look at all the people!" The room in the funeral home was *packed* with people whose lives Bonnie had touched. She touched me when I first applied for a job at the Christian magazine she worked for. Bonnie, as the department administrative coordinator, was the first person I met there, and her warmth and gentleness immediately put me at ease—well, as much at ease as one can be at a job interview. After I got the job we worked closely together. Being the new kid, I would bug her with questions, and she was always patient and always knew the answer. She watched me grow great with child and later came to Amanda's baptism. She loved babies; I almost cried when, at the visitation, her daughter told me that Bonnie kept photos of the baptism up on her refrigerator for weeks. I still have a snapshot of Bonnie leaning over Amanda's crib, smiling at her, giving an infant a gentle little blessing.

She was funny and vital and faithful, and obviously a great many people loved her as I did. Bonnie offered herself, and it was a gift.

But we don't begin and end with ourselves and those we

know. We have Christ's example: "This is how we know what love is: Jesus Christ laid down his life for us. And we ought to lay down our lives for our brothers" (1 John 3:16). (Isn't it interesting how the two John 3:16's complement each other? God so loved us that He sent His Son to give us everlasting life . . . and this is how we are to respond as Christ's followers.)

Part of the Greater Whole

The way of Christ is the way of connection and submission. Even before Christ's coming, God was addressing a people—Israel. Old Testament stories of individuals, such as Abraham, Moses, or David, are part of the larger picture of God's revelation to Israel. Then Christ comes to humankind, and what does He do? Selects disciples. Preaches servanthood. Makes the ultimate sacrifice. After His Resurrection, He sends His Spirit to transform a somewhat motley assembly into . . . a church. And then there are churches, plural, and one apostle God raises up devotes his life to nurturing them and addressing them collectively. And after there are churches, there are (what else?) meetings . . . but *these* meetings are used by the Spirit to come to consensus on some of the foundational doctrines of the faith.

I feel very passionate about this, because I can testify to God's work in my life through other people and the sense of being part of a purpose greater than myself. My connections feel, in the words of a wise colleague, like "the best God has for me."

The first thing that happened after I became a Christian was, I went back to church—where I met the man who would become my husband. I don't believe those were unrelated coincidences. It was as if God was saying, "Together, the two of you can do more for me and my Kingdom than you could each do separately." Fritz introduced me to the books of Catherine Marshall, which spoke of a God intimately involved with our daily lives—a concept I was somewhat fuzzy on at the time. He and I had, and continue to have, many discussions of spiritual things. Our marriage is, in a sense, a workshop—in the words of Walter Wangerin, Jr., a "miniature cathedral"—for living out our faith, a day-to-day environment for walking the talk of forgiveness, sacrificial love, mutual servanthood. We are grateful to have been given a good marriage when so many struggle; but we also feel that God means for us to use this gift as part of a greater plan, to somehow share ourselves with others.

And I'll never forget our first visit to what is now our church home. We had been church shopping for nearly three years. For a few months we might land in one place, but it never felt quite right; we'd be driving home after worship and say things like, "Good sermon," but we both knew we were missing something.

We were friends with several people who went to one particular church. We hadn't tried it because it was a distance away (or so it seemed) and the 9:30 service seemed awfully early for slugabeds, such as myself. But one summer morning we decided to give it a try. The greeting couple welcomed us enthusiastically, as if we were already friends. When we entered the sanctuary a man we already knew spotted us and boomed out a stage whisper, "Fritz!" People were dressed casually and seemed at ease. We sat in front of another couple of our acquaintance, and the husband leaned forward and whispered, laughing, "They make visitors stand up and tell all about themselves." The assistant pastor (the husband of my musician friend) preached on the gift of sex in marriage. The music was an unusual blend of contemporary and traditional, which appealed to us. Most of all, it felt like a *community* instead of an audience.

We knew, then, that our search was over.

Then there's the part of my life that can feel isolated—those of you who work at home will know what I mean, especially if your kids are at school and your husband at work all day. I love to write, but it's a solitary pursuit, me and my computer. Sometimes I don't even answer the phone when

I don't want distractions. (I started using my answering machine after an incident when the phone rang. I was working, and my foot had fallen asleep. So I sort of lurched to the phone, going, "Hold on!" and picked up and a heavily accented voice said, "Eez thees Meesus Smeeth?")

It's especially challenging for me because I'm energized by people and attention and conversation—I can relate to what C.S. Lewis once said, that if he had to choose between giving up writing and giving up friendships, he would give up writing.

I can relate to what C. S. Lewis once said, that if he had to choose between giving up writing and giving up friendships, he would give up writing.

What keeps me going, aside from my family and friends and getting out to speak every now and then, is the sense that *you*, a friend I've never met, are out there, and there are things I want to say to you, and that together we, too, comprise a few cells in the Body. What keeps me going are little glimmers of encouragement, such as the letter I received just the other day from a young mom in England who had read *Sometimes I Feel Like Running Away From Home*—twice—and took the time to tell me how it had helped her. I used to have a lot of pen pals when I was a teenager, and seeing that foreign airmail envelope in the mail absolutely made my day.

The opposite—no Body, no connection—is too dreadful to contemplate. Novelist Randy Alcorn, in his book *Deadline*, the story of a contemporary journalist whose friends' deaths in a mysterious car accident lead him on a search for answers both factual (what killed them?) and spiritual (is there, after all, a God and is His name Jesus?), creates intriguing pictures of the afterlife that the two friends find themselves in. One, a Christian, discovers heaven to be a place of unending joy, a place where he encounters powerful warriors of light who serve as guardian angels. The other, a prominent surgeon who performed abortions and rejected efforts to bring him to Christ, goes . . . elsewhere. In this place, he is entirely alone. He had always imagined hell to be a place where all the sinners hang out together, having a sinful sort of revelry, whereas in heaven all the denizens wear long faces and have to listen to harp music all—I almost said "day," but you see what I mean. Instead he is lost in eternal black silence.

Perhaps each of us in the end stands alone before God to account for our lives, but I can't help but think that somewhere in a celestial antechamber, there will be people waiting to ask us, "How did it go?"

We don't really know what awaits us, of course—except that if we confess that Christ is Lord, *He* will be waiting for us. And I believe that our friends and family who have also yielded to Christ and lived accordingly will be there to welcome us. What I find unimaginably horrifying is a fate of permanent solitude, with only myself for company. That, to me, feels like absolute damnation.

The way of Christ is the way of connectedness. Perhaps each of us in the end stands alone before God to account for our lives, but I can't help but think that somewhere in a celestial antechamber, there will be people waiting to ask us, "How did it go?" And if it went well, those people will have played a mighty part.

11

Someone to Help You Up

OF COURSE, BEFORE THAT great day comes, we have our responsibilities here below. We need others not only for companionship and connection, but because relationships, when they work as God intended, can bring out the best in us. We become more unselfish, more empathetic, more honest and accepting, and even truer to ourselves.

Jesus brought out the best in others. In impetuous Simon Peter, He saw an energy and passion and potential for leadership that would serve the Kingdom well. Jesus looked past the surface of Matthew, the despised tax collector, of Mary Magdalene, the loose woman, of Martha, the harried housewife who I imagine could have been something of a scold, even reproving the Master ("Why didn't you come right away?").

But the example of Jesus that speaks most forcefully to me is the time He spent with Nicodemus, explaining the Truth to him. It's easy for me—and I think for many of us— to feel compassion for those who seem needy and struggling. But who reaches out to those who seem to have it all— money, status, professional renown? Who sees beyond the facade? Jesus did. He could have dismissed Nicodemus as another know-it-all Pharisee. But He saw beneath the rich robes and perceived a soul searching for answers.

Whatever our situation, we can bring out the best in others by allowing *them* to be Christ for us.

When Our Resources Dry Up

A friend and I were once talking about this. We agreed that there are times when we can feel so depressed, so discouraged, that a sort of paralysis sets in. It's a paradox: When we're feeling pretty good, we have the energy to help ourselves. When we're feeling down, we don't.

Maybe you've had the same experience. You *know* you'd feel better if you got some exercise, read the Bible, got involved in some work that took you out of yourself. You *know* you should pray. But you can't even muster the energy to talk to God (and anyway, you're not feeling that great about Him at the moment).

I can recognize the signs in myself right away. I waste time. I stay up too late. I snack. I ignore my to-do list . . . why bother?

At these times, we can identify with the poor beetle on the sidewalk, thrashing its legs, unable to get up without assistance. This is where other people step in. You know that old poem "Footprints in the Sand"? It speaks of the times God carries us. Many of those times, I believe, God uses the arms of His Body to do the carrying. We can come to a place where our own resources simply run out, when we're too wounded to move.

But we still, somehow, have to reach out with those thrashing legs. People can't always guess when we need them. In Chapter 8, on finding God in the everyday, I talked about those bustling Marthas who look like the busiest of the Lord's servants, but inside they're dry holes. Often people who feel like this are too proud to ask for help, because it seems weak and threatens their own image of themselves as capable and independent. I've known a few women who brought needless suffering upon themselves because of their unwillingness to bend, to reveal a crack in the all-competent facade. But our selves are *not* sufficient. Sometimes, the greatest gift we can give people is the gift of our dependency.

Sometimes, the greatest gift we can give people is the gift of our dependency.

Asking for Help

There have been a few times when I've asked Amanda to help me with something. Now that she's eleven, I'm finding that there are things she's better at than I am (and if *that* isn't a humbling experience . . .). She's a great folder, for instance. I'm okay, but she could arrange displays for Linens 'n Things. When I say to her, "Honey, would you mind helping me rearrange this closet? You're better at it than I am," she just sparkles. (It makes me wonder if we're making our older children feel useful enough in the family enterprise— not in the sense of "teaching them to do chores," but because it's a basic human need to feel as if one can *contribute* to something larger.)

Our dependency can take a spiritual form. I don't always love God as completely and *surely* as I should. I have days when I just feel so confident and connected to Him, really on fire for the Lord, that I want to help others and share my joy. There are other times, however, when I don't feel very confident, when anxiety and irritation get the better of me and all I want to do is share my misery and have people feel sorry for me. It's then I'm eternally grateful for the presence, encouragement, and, especially, the *example* of others—

even the example of a friend who says, "Yeah, I felt crabby and ugly just the other day, so I finished off the pie in the refrigerator and then felt even worse!"

My pastor said something in a sermon I wrote down word for word. "When we go one on one with the adversary," he observed, "we're always going to lose." But when others, equipped with the armor of Christ—including the armor of laughter and empathy—bolster our defenses, Satan is kept on the outside looking in.

Passing It On

We don't have to have tons of friends—indeed, it's better if we don't run around telling everyone our woes. The best thing we can do is have a few people in our lives—beyond our spouses or mothers—to whom we can come "just as we are," people who *get it*, people with whom we can share both our struggles and victories (the latter are harder to find), people who are relatively mature Christians. People who are, in a phrase I saw somewhere, "like-souled."

To pray regularly with and for another person not only cements a relationship, but I think it exponentially increases the Spirit's power. To know that my prayer partner, Barb, is interceding in my behalf makes me feel like I have a cheerleader before God. You know how people come and go from our prayer lists? I'm a permanent resident on Barb's list, and she on mine.

Barb can come to me and say, in effect, "I'm a mess; I need help." She knows I won't judge her or schedule her for two weeks from today or pretend that I've never been a mess. She knows. Once when she was out delivering Meals on Wheels, she had to make a phone call to find an address. She stopped by my house just before noon. Naturally, it was the one day when I hadn't gotten dressed, hadn't cleaned up, hadn't done anything except write. It occurs to me that we should all make a habit of dropping in on our friends un-expectedly—just once—so we can get over this idea that everybody is perfect except us.

When we have friends like this, we don't have to reach very far to be lifted up. In the "Wrestling with Angels" video series on tough issues Christians face, a woman named Ann spoke of her feelings of abandonment: "Everyone has someone who's more important than me . . . nobody hangs around." Then a friend said to her, "It only takes one person—and I love you and will give that to you."

We should all make a habit of dropping in on our friends unexpectedly—just once—so we can get over this idea that everybody is perfect except us.

And then, God's desire is that lonely Ann should, in turn, pass that on to someone else. This self-offering is a sacred obligation. Oswald Chambers says it with his usual succinctness: "The thing that astonishes us when we get through to God is the way God holds us responsible for other lives."[1] When God gives us the gift of salvation in Christ, we are *required* to share the gift with others, to exhibit the fruits of a changed life.

What Are We Waiting For?

I keep thinking about Jesus' words about losing and finding our lives for His sake. Most of us put it backward: First I'll find myself, figure out what I'm all about, learn to like myself and generally clean up my act—then I'll be ready to help others.

That's kind of like refusing to let anyone into your house until it looks like Martha Stewart (how'd she get in here?) is your personal maid. As with contentment, we never completely *arrive* at a state of complete self-knowledge and unwavering self-confidence. The notion reminds me of some Zen mystic, retreating to a cave to find bliss. One of the things I love about Christianity is it's such a rubbing-elbows, in-the-thick-of-things kind of—I almost said "faith," but let's call it life—with supreme relevance to every aspect of our existence. You say you love other people? Show it. You say you've been given a gift? Use it. You say you know Christ as your Savior? Share it.

Even in the midst of our own struggles, we can jump into that fray. When I think of the most compassionate people I know, those who are quickest to reach out, those whom God is using, I realize that nearly all of them have endured some suffering, may still *be* suffering. Today I reread 2 Corinthians 10–13 and was really struck by Paul's openness about himself and his struggles, his almost desperate urgency to communicate the truth to the straying church *through* his weakness, not in spite of it. It occurs to me that God intends for all of us to "boast all the more gladly about [our] weaknesses, so that Christ's power may rest on [us]" (12:9).

Boy, this is hard to do. We'd much prefer to help someone from a "superior" position and not boast about our weaknesses—and, too, have you ever thought about the idea that we can fall into the "I'm-more-open-than-you-are" trap? (I hadn't either, until I heard a Christian counselor bring it up in a meeting. I think there's something to it.) But the goal is not *our* power, it's "Christ's power" resting on us. And if God intends to use our frailties, they will be used, even through our prideful resistance to the idea. I've had the experience of speaking and thinking I was coming across as really put together, until someone came up to me afterward and said, "You're so much like the rest of us. I like that."

And When a Friend *Doesn't* Help . . .

Relationships can also bring us closer to Christ in that we recognize our own limitations when it comes to helping others. I'm involved in a situation right now where a friend of mine is really hurting—big-time. I can do small things for her; I can make suggestions; I can pray for her and be there for her, but I can't make the pain go away. It's too big to be relieved by a friendly chat. I can help her up—but only Christ can keep her there, and I have to trust Him to keep her in the palm of His hand.

I can help her up—but only Christ can keep her there, and I have to trust Him to keep her in the palm of His hand.

And, of course, not every relationship models Christlikeness. There are, sadly, people who can draw us away from God, people who bring out the worst in us. You know, the person who, if you're having a good day, can ruin that day. I know one individual like this. I don't want to say very much or even identify whether they're a man or a woman, but this person just makes me feel *bad*. I don't know if it's because I see the worst of myself in them, or because this person, for some weird reason, is trying to subtly undermine me, but it's there, and it's occurred to me to wonder whether this person feels the same way about me.

We all have similar stories. There's the endlessly needy acquaintance who can almost suffocate us emotionally; the so-called friend we can never depend on; the parent or sibling who can undermine our hard-won growth and maturity and make us feel like we're fifteen again. I've even heard really sad stories of women who felt this way about one of their grown children.

But God can use even these challenges to spur us on in our walk with Him, to help us look at ourselves honestly in the light of Psalm 139:

- Do I secretly enjoy another's dependence because it makes me feel superior?
- Am I as reliable a friend as I could be?
- Are there unresolved issues from my past I should be sorting out?
- Should I confront this person or just shake the dust off my feet and move on?
- Does he or she need me to share the love of Christ with them?

I believe it was Dietrich Bonhoeffer, the martyred German theologian, who called Jesus "the man for others." To be the *person* for others seems to me to be a very high calling, even if we're not out there doing great things for the Lord (or so we think). There's a song that talks about forgetting about ourselves and magnifying the Lord. Too much emphasis on self keeps us from true worship. When I'm too concerned with *my* self, *my* needs—that's when I can feel separated from God. When Billy Graham says that solutions to society's problems start with a change in the human heart, I think what he's getting at is that we all need a little less "me" and a little more "we"; a little less selfishness and a lot more love and willingness to extend ourselves for the sake of others—as Christ did, all the way to the Cross.

Thinking about the Cross—and what happened afterward—makes me think about that one time in the year when it feels like everything comes together, that this is what we've all been working and waiting for. That's on Easter Sunday. I always get up a little early to have some time to contemplate what Jesus did for me with His death and His rising, but going to church puts flesh on that gift. We dress in our best, whatever the weather (which is usually a disappointment), get to church early to get a good seat, and everyone else is dressed in *their* best. And we sing the first hymn, which had better be "Christ the Lord Is Risen Today" or somebody will hear about it . . . and I'm singing all the verses without looking at the hymnal: "Soar we now where

Christ has led, Alleluia! Following our exalted Head . . ."
And I look around and a lot of other people are singing from
the heart, and it feels so good to be saying "soar we," instead
of "soar I." Somehow, it just rings true.

Notes

1. *Oswald Chambers: The Best From All His Books, Volume
   II*, edited by Harry Verploegh (Thomas Nelson, 1989), p.
   263.

12

Come to the Feast—
and Don't Skip Dessert!

WE'VE TALKED ABOUT PAWING THROUGH the drawers of our lives, looking for God amid the clutter. We've talked about ways He might work through our lives. But let's back away from the clutter for a moment. Let's stop being so grim and forget about work entirely. Let's think about *delight*.

One of my favorite Communion liturgies proclaims, "Friends, this is the joyful feast of the Lord!" A banquet. A come-as-you-are party, with Christ presiding over the table, delighting in our presence.

We can forget that sometimes God just wants to delight us. To play with us, really. Look at giraffes and shooting stars, at platypuses and stalactites. Look at those lizards you see skipping across the water on those public-TV nature shows.

For some reason, this delight can be hard for me to accept. I understand God as the stern Parent, God as the all-powerful Creator, God as the sorrowing Comforter. But there's another side of God that, because most of us are at a stage of life where we have to be serious and "responsible," we can dismiss. We find it hard to accept because in our adult world, hardly anybody gives us something for nothing. We're forever having to prove ourselves, earn our keep, justify our existence. Even our relationships have an element of tit for tat in them—who among us loves someone who never loves us back? Oh, every now and then our spouse, for example, may give us a gift "just because." More often, though—even in the best marriages—we have to remind our mates that it sure would be nice to get taken out to dinner, preferably at a place without a drive-up window.

God doesn't have to be reminded that we might feel hurt if we weren't invited to His joyful feast. He really wants us there! It's the God who tugs on our sleeves and says, "Catch Me if you can!" It's God as the Lord of the Dance. And we don't have to wear the right clothes or join the right groups or do much of anything to earn that invitation.

A Breath of Delight

In my experience, God often comes at us indirectly, obliquely, with these moments of delight, something like glimpsing a rare bird out of the corner of our eye. It happened to me once when I was out for a walk. It was one of the two best times of the year, late May/early June. (The other best time is October, the month I was born in.) The leaves are new and green, the world seems fresh-washed, the last vestiges of winter have been banished, and the trees are full of birdsong. As a bonus, every now and then you get some really interesting thunderstorms. I glanced at the puffy, harmless clouds riding the western horizon and suddenly—it must have been some trick of the light or breath of wind—I remembered June mornings when I was six or seven and just out of school. I don't normally daydream so intensely I lose track of where I am, but it happened this time. Powerful memories and long-forgotten images rose up: the breeze blowing through the open windows, strawberries with my Grape-Nuts Flakes, milk from the milkman, sneakers instead of saddle shoes, and me looking at the western sky, toward what was then still semi-open country, and having a shivering sense of a vast and uncharted land, dappled by cloud-shadows.

The sensation was so strong I felt a tear welling up—for my lost childhood, for the lost countryside that has in so many places been paved over, but also for sheer gratitude and joy: What a beautiful world this was and is and will be! It was a feeling of both longing and having, of past wonders and future possibilities. I really wanted to go frolicking down Forest Avenue, twirling my skirt like I did as a little girl. Of course, I was afraid of what the neighbors would think. But I think I went twirling inwardly, and I hope God understood.

I'm aware of the dangers of ascribing subjective experience to God. But every time something like this happens to me it feels so . . . *true*, so close to who I am, and so really wonderful and out of the ordinary that I have to allow for the possibility that the Lord was revealing to me yet another side of himself, that He was saying, "Here, child, is a glimpse of things I know you love. I do this that you might be encouraged to continue seeking Me and all I have to offer you. I do this to delight you."

God's Personal Touch

Certainly there is a general revelation of God—through the Word, through the sacraments our Lord instituted, through the experience of communal worship. Maybe, though, God wants so much to reach each of us that He may approach us through very specific, almost tailor-made means, and that approach may vary according to the particular point of need in our lives and the language we understand best. Notice in the Gospels how Jesus is by turns probing (as with the Samaritan woman), compassionate (the woman who anointed His feet), even lighthearted (He must have grinned at little Zacchaeus peering down from the tree!).

I think I know how Zacchaeus felt, wanting so much to see Jesus that he perched in the sycamore. I've had the same desire, only I was looking up. It happens every spring when this one particular flock of birds—I think they're sandhill cranes—passes over, wheeling and calling way, way up in the sky on their way to Wisconsin waters. It's always at the same time of day, around noon. They're so high they look like little floating commas, a whole bunch of them, curving together and then drifting apart. When I hear their cry, I drop everything and run outdoors and stare and stare until I feel as if I, too, would somehow get whisked up into the blue. If I were to put my response into words, it would be something like, *Cranes! Praise God!*

God knows I love things like birds and clouds, so He uses these means to get through to me. He may use other means to get through to you. God is incredibly personal. I know people for whom music is the language of the angels, people who connect strongly with God through teaching children, people who feel closest to Him when they work with their hands on something satisfying. I've heard of Christian scientists who see God in the beauty of physics or astronomy or even mathematics. God may call you through a special memory or cherished dream. But through all these doors, the Lord of the Dance beckons to each of us and says, "Come."

There are times when God opens a door we weren't even looking at. You know how we get these stereotypes about ourselves: "I'm an introvert"; "I'm not mechanical"; that kind of thing. Well, I have to confess, I've never thought of myself as being very intellectual about the Bible. I have always responded to it on a devotional or emotional level (what does this Scripture say about my life?) or as story (so then what did David do?). Questions of history, terminology, and various practices did not seem very relevant to me, though I respected others' expertise in these areas.

Then I was asked to help edit a study Bible that stressed these very issues. I thought, *Why not? Might be an interesting challenge, and it's kind of a compliment to be asked.*

It was hard work—I expected that. What I did not expect was how reviewing scholarly research drew me further into God's Word, into the details as well as the big picture. I learned why the details matter. I found I loved digging into the text, learning new facts, discovering hitherto unknown treasures of the Word—revering Scripture for itself, not just for what it says to me. It was also, I think, God gently reminding me that subjective experience must be balanced by a grounding in the facts: Where is it written—or, more to the point, where have *I* written it?

I don't think I'll ever become a Bible scholar. It really isn't my gift. But the work gave me that same feeling of delight and discovery, of God—I don't want to say, "sneaking up on me," but of Him taking me by surprise. There are all kinds of ways to dance.

God will not be limited: Who would imagine Him speaking in a "gentle whisper" (1 Kings 19:12), when He could arrive in an earthquake?

Elijah, of course, had been alerted to the Lord's coming. The Almighty himself had told him, "The Lord is about to pass by" (v. 11). God doesn't usually herald himself to us in this way. Klyne Snodgrass, writing in *Between Two Truths*, speculates that God may often remain hidden from us because "for God to have authentic relations with people, there must be freedom. . . . God does not coerce; He invites."[1] (There's that word again: *invites*.) But He is with us nonetheless! Promise after promise in Scripture attests to His presence and activity among us. These signs of God I have described may not be direct revelation (I leave it to theologians to argue about dispensations and such). But they're little reminders, gentle elbowings from God to appreciate His gifts, to look up from the clutter and into the sky, to keep my eyes open to the possibility that He might, after all, be passing by.

Does Work Love You Back?

Are you struggling with this? Do you long for God to show himself—somehow, somewhere? Do you feel as if you've become dulled to the possibility of His presence, and you wonder where the joy is?

I can certainly relate. I admire people who are natural optimists. I know one man whose answering machine message proclaims, "Praise the Lord! You've reached . . ." There are days when I'd like to record a message that says, "I know you're probably trying to sell me something and I don't want to talk to you. So at the sound of the beep, hang up." I'm NOT one of those perky people who makes lemonade out of lemons. I'm more likely to squinch up my face and go, "Eeew, I wanted oranges."

I used to think that optimists were hopelessly out of touch with reality and pessimists astute observers of the human condition. And if you look only at the *world*—at least that public part of the world that we're all aware of—the pessimists win hands down. But just because we live among muck doesn't mean we have to get down and roll in it. It's scary how easy it is to get pulled into negative attitudes, unthinkingly critical responses. To lose sight of the joy that Christ alone extends to us. To stop playing.

We've already spoken about "finding God in the everyday," about slowing down and giving our souls the space they need to stretch and grow, rather than being all tight and contracted. In addition to slowing down, we need to play more, to do things that aren't necessarily productive or meaningful.

I mentioned the women's group we're forming at church. As with many women's groups, everyone comes with a different need, so we've been discussing a combination of meeting in a large group and also breaking down into small, interest-based circles. The one that jumped out at me was a "fun" group that would focus on such amusements as seeing one of those weeper "chick" movies, getting together at someone's house and cooking an ethnic meal, or attending a concert or ball game. I did not want to have an intense sharing experience or be in a Bible study or book discussion group. Sometimes I feel as if I'm overdosing on meaningful activities. When was the last time you saw a movie that really took you out of yourself? When was the last time you just fell over laughing with friends, read a long and wholesomely romantic novel like those offered by this publisher, played a heated game of Monopoly, or threw autumn leaves around? When was the last time you enjoyed some shallow pleasure and didn't feel guilty about it?

Sometimes I feel as if I'm overdosing on meaningful activities.

I saw a Labor Day related news story once about a man who hadn't missed a day of work in fifty years. I can't remember what his job was, but it wasn't anything especially absorbing and varied like, say, being a country doctor. He may have worked for the post office or some insurance company. Anyway, I saw that story and while I admired his devotion to duty, I questioned his sense of what matters in life. (I also wondered if he sometimes showed up coughing and sneezing all over his workmates. What are the odds that a person will never get sick even once in fifty years?)

I know we all have to work harder and longer to keep up. And don't think that those of us who work at home have it easy. Lately—and this is one of the hidden traps of working at home, because the work is always there—I find myself spending some part of every day except Sunday working. My work gives me pleasure, but not always. There's that feeling of having to produce to demonstrate my value. And when I'm not working I'm trying to keep up with my house and family and church stuff. I have a stack of books on my desk I would love to read, Chaim Potok and Amy Tan and Garrison Keillor and a bunch of others. That's play for me, too, but right now there isn't a lot of time for that. And it makes me wonder what all this emphasis on work does to our spirits. Are we human beings, or just units of production? Does work love you back? Not always. Ask all the men and women who have been laid off in recent years.

"Christian" work can weigh us down in the same way. Charles Swindoll quotes a writer named Jim McGuiggan: "Some saints can't enjoy a meal because the world is starving. . . . They are afraid to smile because of the world's sadness. . . . They know nothing of balance. And they're miserable because of it. They have no inner incentive to bring people into a relationship with Christ which would make them feel as miserable as they themselves feel."[2] Most of us wouldn't go as far as these suffering saints, but you see the point. Our Christian work, our church involvements, can feel like obligation. We can think we're wasting time unless we're doing something edifying and constructive, something to make us a "better person."

When was the last time you enjoyed some shallow pleasure and didn't feel guilty about it?

Parenting doesn't always have to be work, either. When we're with our kids, we don't always have to be searching for that teachable moment. (Unrelated non-sequitur story here: Sometimes the teachable moment finds us. I was reading a story to Amanda about a girl from medieval times whose brother had gone on the Crusades. I explained what the Crusades were and somehow the conversation strayed into theology. "Mom," she asked, "were there dinosaurs in Adam and Eve times?" I gave some hedging answer about how God created everything and told her to ask her Sunday-school teacher. Linda's a trial lawyer; I'm sure she can come up with a convincing response.)

We can just get silly with our children, join in their laughter, make stupid jokes. We can get silly with our spouses—I just read an article in _Marriage Partnership_ magazine where the writer, Randy Frame, told of entertaining his bride, Jeron, by having a grape-tossing contest with his brother. As in, each was trying to toss a grape into the other's mouth. (I know Randy, and the image fits.)

Getting Away . . . for a While

You know, "escapism" has gotten a bad name in our culture. We equate it with unhealthy fantasy or frittering away time and money on trivial entertainment, like the riverboat casino I mentioned earlier. But it's equally unhealthy to _always_ focus on ourselves and our problems, to do nothing but work, to never lose ourselves in something delightful and different and insignificant. Play can put things in perspective, reminding us that not everything—ourselves included—has cosmic import. It also frees our minds to think creatively, even whimsically; it keeps us "loose," in sports jargon. I remember once we were watching the Chicago Bulls play some particularly hapless opponent. They were way ahead, and they just started having fun—playfully passing, sometimes missing shots, grinning at each other. They were truly _playing_ basketball, and it was really refreshing in an era when so many athletes seem so grim.

Besides, life is just so hard sometimes. Why _not_ escape, if only for a little while? Play, fun, laughter can help release the tensions and toxins that can build up inside us. Has it ever happened to you that you were really enjoying yourself, maybe playing some silly game, and the thought came to you: *Boy, I really needed this! Why don't I do this more often?*

Play can put things in perspective, reminding us that not everything—ourselves included— has cosmic import.

I've heard some Christians distinguish between "pleasure" and "joy." Pleasure, they say, is temporary and not to be pursued, because it will always elude you. Joy comes from God and is within you no matter what. I agree, sort of. Life shouldn't be focused on pleasure alone. But I think certain *kinds* of pleasure can be a gateway to apprehending joy—can open the door to that feast of the Lord. And when we're not enjoying our lives very much, it's hard to feel we have a place at that Table.

It's been said that a Puritan is someone who's deathly afraid that somebody, somewhere, might be enjoying himself. What a corruption of what God intends for us! I much prefer John Fischer's approach. He once wrote a book titled *Real Christians Don't Dance*, with an "x" over the "don't." Real Christians dance! Real Christians are free to laugh boisterously, to have grape-tossing contests, to occasionally say, "I'm going to order the banana cream pie for dessert AND I DON'T CARE," to rescue stranded earthworms from sidewalks after a rain (yeah, that's me out there).

Real Christians can kick out the toxins and thumb their

noses at that prune-faced Puritan. Let her go do something useful like organize her closets. We've got a banquet to get to.

Notes

1. Klyne Snodgrass, *Between Two Truths: Living With Biblical Tensions* (Zondervan, 1990), p. 145.
2. From *The Irish Papers*, cited in Charles R. Swindoll, *Laugh Again* (Waco, Tex.: Word, 1991), p. 104.

13

Jumping into Niagara Falls

ONE SUNDAY MORNING, after speaking at a retreat in Buffalo, New York, I was treated to a picture of God that has stayed with me ever since. As our plane took off, the captain—a young woman—announced over the P.A. system that we would be circling over Niagara Falls. (I have a feeling she took us out of her way to show us the spectacle. I wonder if a man would have done the same thing. Or would he have kept directly to his flight plan, probably right over an industrial park?)

The day was clear, with almost unlimited visibility. Passengers peered out the windows. Suddenly—there it was! The jet dipped a little lower. There was the entire crescent of the falls, both American and Canadian. I could almost hear the roar. The sun shone bright on the foam and the froth. As the captain slowly circled the plane, we could see the river, the falls, the Great Lake—an entire amazing aquatic geography.

This was not my first encounter with Niagara. My husband and I stopped there years ago. I still remember the boom of the water, the rainbows, the incredible sense of danger. I did not want to take *The Maid of the Mist* tour boat.

But I sure wanted to look, listen, and marvel.

The life God offers us reminds me of Niagara. Huge. Awesome. Never-ending, impossible abundance. And . . . a little scary. Maybe even a lot scary.

We've been looking at how to lift our eyes from the clutter, how to seek God *in* the clutter, starting where we are. But eventually, we have to do more than take little steps. We have to take a great big leap.

Too many of us, too much of the time, live safe and small. You know what it reminds me of? It reminds me of someone trying to get a drink from a trickling hose, trying to wrench more water out of a recalcitrant outdoor faucet—while behind us, Niagara booms away.

Too many of us live safe and small . . . as if we're trying to get a drink from a trickling hose, while behind us, Niagara booms away.

In Ephesians 3:20, Paul speaks of "him who is able to do immeasurably more than all we ask or imagine, according to his power that is at work within us." Do we believe that? Do we live like we believe it?

There will be showers of blessing—torrents, tsunamis, deluges of blessing! More than trickles and drips. God wants to pour His Living Water out on us.

But if we want to go deep into that water, we have to go deep with Him. We need that "one holy passion, filling all my frame" that the old hymn speaks of—the passion to know God, to love Him, to serve Him, to be used by Him. And we can't limit God.

We limit God when we think, *But I'm nobody special; I have no real talents; I'm not a writer or speaker or musician or athlete or whatever. I don't want to lead anybody or go to* _the mission field. Besides, I'm too busy. I'll get to God after my kids are grown and launched. I'll stand in those showers of blessing after I've gotten my own act together. There're chores and commitments and well, just life. I'm doing all right. It'll do._

But life is from God. "It'll do" isn't enough.

Are we making the most of these lives we've been given? Do we know anyone who is?

Life is from God. "It'll do" isn't enough.

Role Models

You know, one good role model can fire the imagination better than a thousand words of preaching. When my daughter balks at practicing her cello, I remind her that Michael Jordan, for all his incredible abilities, also has an estimable work ethic. He practices doggedly, daily. Always trying to get better. Working on the fundamentals. He could just show up and collect his enormous paycheck, but pride and love of the game keep him going. And she wants to be like Mike, so she practices. In the same way, there are Christians who seem to be fully living the life God gave them—role models for grownups, if you will.

A while back we went to see Ken Medema in concert. What an evening! The problem I have with a lot of contemporary Christian music (actually, a lot of contemporary music, period) is, it's so _bland_, so packaged-sounding. Too many singers sound the same. Little tinkly synthesizers. Safe and predictable. But Ken Medema is to the tinkly-synthesizer music as Niagara is to the hose trickle. He fairly explodes off the stage with passion for communicating something of his excitement about God. You can't pigeonhole what he does; it's rock and gospel and jazz and classical, wrapped around lyrics that come close to poetry. And he's got something I don't see enough of in Christian music: a sense of humor. I mean, the guy's hilarious.

When I watched him on the church platform I imagined he was this huge and powerful spellbinder. But afterward, seeing him greet people in the lobby outside the church auditorium, I realized he was just an ordinary-sized, tired-looking middle-aged man. I can only imagine how drained he must have been after two hours of totally giving himself in performance, but he patiently talked to everyone who approached him, touching infants, kneeling down to speak with children. He wasn't autographing anything; he wasn't surrounded by "handlers." I thought, *There is a man who lives with God.*

The amazing thing is, Ken Medema is blind. He will never see a child's face or marvel at the sun shining on Niagara's foam. He sang a song that made me cry, about getting to heaven and seeing Jesus. But his example makes me feel small and careful and crabbed, throwing up unnecessary roadblocks on my journey with Christ. What's *my* excuse? Ken Medema has gone to the limits with the gifts God has given him, and he uses those considerable gifts to share the wonder that is life in Christ. I am quite certain that Ken Medema spends a great deal of time drawing on the Living Water—through prayer in solitude and perhaps with intimate others, through time spent in the Word, through worship. He gives so much, he would *have* to. But I also suspect Ken doesn't limit God. As a person with a disability, Ken would know something about being confined in a box. He's broken out of that box—and he doesn't keep God in one, either.

I want to be like Ken. I hardly have his talents, but I want to take whatever I've been given and do something with it. I want to go the limit with God.

With God All Things ARE Possible!

We hear the Annunciation story every Advent. For many of us this is one of the most winsome narratives in Scripture. Here this angel just shows up at Mary's door—I picture her spinning or sweeping or making bread—and says, "Surprise! You're going to give birth to God!" I don't know what I'd do. To tell you the truth, it's wonderful and inspiring to *read* about angels, but I'm not sure I really want to *see* one, not on earth. Give Mary credit. She isn't sure ("How can this be?"), but she doesn't argue. She says, in effect, "Okay. I'm in the Lord's hands. I'll do it."

It seems to me that one of the hallmarks of those who want to go the limit with God is the openness to say, "Okay. I'll do it. I'll go as far as you want to take me." They understand that there are all kinds of ways that God can act, all kinds of people God can use. They *want* to be surprised. They relish challenges.

One of the hallmarks of those who want to go the limit with God is the openness to say, "Okay. I'll do it. I'll go as far as you want to take me."

My sister keeps up with contemporary stuff a lot better than I do. Maybe it's because she's twelve years younger than I am and lives just across the Hudson River from the Manhattan skyline, whereas I'm . . . twelve years older and live just across Forest Avenue from the room addition our neighbors are building. Anyway, she uses a phrase I like: "Livin' large!" She tends to apply it sarcastically (like when you decide to have a Coke instead of just water), but the idea of "livin' large" appeals to me. Especially living large in God.

The Current of Life

It has to be more than just an attitude. It's easier to open up that box many of us keep God in if we have the right tools, easier to draw on "the power at work within us" if we're connected to the current. We haven't said much about prayer, and I want to rectify that right now. When we pray, we're sampling the Living Water and opening ourselves up to greater Niagaras. (Speaking of which, I've been surprised by how many women—and no men—have told me they pray in the shower.)

As busy as we may be, I'm learning that skimping on prayer is truly a false economy. I ALWAYS feel better after I pray, especially my jump-start morning prayer. It gets back to that idea of filling the tank and then sharing the overflow with others: It's energizing.

I've noticed that when I'm feeling disconnected to the current, my prayers shrink and concern mostly myself and a faint hope that somehow God will help me with some immediate problem. Or I dutifully pray through some list. But if we believe that God is great and all-powerful and loves us beyond our wildest imaginings, we need to be praying boldly, not tentatively—to "live large" in our address to God.

Is there something you've been longing for, but you've never been able to see how it could happen? Ask! Put it out there before God. *You* can't see how it can happen. *He* can. Give Him credit for making the seemingly impossible possible. Be persistent, like the man wanting to borrow three loaves of bread at midnight or the widow seeking justice.

I've been praying for a couple of *years* now about a book I want to write that hasn't yet found a publisher. There's really nothing more I can do to sell the project. But I feel strongly about its message and have received a number of confirmations that I'm on the right track, so I'm not giving up, even in the face of rejection. I have confidence that somehow God will open the door for this project to become a reality. It's a big prayer, but then God is much, much bigger.

And we can pray similarly large prayers for others. My daughter will be entering high school in . . . can it be? . . . three years. The public high school is all right, but there's also a fine Christian prep school a couple of towns away, and this idea keeps nagging at me that Amanda should go there. On the face of it, it sounds like an impossible dream—the school is expensive, our property taxes are high as it is, I'd probably have to go out and get a real job to help pay the tuition . . . objections, objections. But I'm starting to lay this prayer, too, at God's feet.

Remember the friend I mentioned, the one who is really hurting? If I look realistically at her situation, I can't see a solution. But again, *God* can. So I continue to lift her up to Him, almost challenging Him to do the amazing.

Don't Get Left Behind

It's so easy to get trapped in the immediate reality of our day-to-day existence. I think of C. S. Lewis's *The Last Battle*,[1] the final story in *The Chronicles of Narnia*. The Pevensies and Eustace and Jill discover themselves in a place that looks a lot like heaven. Narnia is coming to an end, but Aslan is leading them "further up and further in," exploring the wondrous new world. Meanwhile, the Dwarfs remain just inside the doorway that leads from the old, dying world into the new, sitting with their backs turned, refusing to join the journey. They're limited to their own little group, their own stunted little world. And they're left behind.

But we don't have to be. We *already*, according to Paul, have "his power that is at work within [us]." Within *you*. That's God's power, and we need to believe in it and draw upon it. But His power is inseparable from His love. Go back a couple of verses and listen to Paul: "I pray that out of his glorious riches he may strengthen you with power through his Spirit in your inner being, so that Christ may dwell in your hearts through faith. And I pray that you, being rooted and established in love, may have power, together with all the saints, to grasp how wide and long and high and deep is the love of Christ, and to know this love that surpasses knowledge—that you may be filled to the measure of all the fullness of God" (Ephesians 3:16–19).

Think about that for a moment. Wide and long and high and deep, like the ocean or an endless horizon. So wide and so long that it can reach down to you and encircle you. And it knows your name.

The God who created Niagara Falls also has a very personal and particular love for you. It isn't an abstract love. For "God so loved the world" we could also substitute "God so loved Betsey" or "God so loved Fritz" or whatever your name happens to be.

He made you, and that is a wonder. So . . . don't limit God. With Him, all things *are* possible. He may not respond the way we want—then again, He may well give us our heart's desire. He may challenge us to do something very hard. He may startle us. I never thought I could speak in public—I would have put it on my list alongside unanesthetized gum surgery as one of my least favorite pastimes. Ha! Now I'll do it anywhere, anytime. I'm not afraid of it, and, while I'm no Chuck (or Luci) Swindoll, I know I don't put my audiences to sleep. Don't limit God.

He made you, and that is a wonder. So . . . don't limit God.

What is God, incarnate in Christ, holding out to *you* today? A child? A challenge to use the gifts He has given you? A chance for forgiveness in a relationship you thought irretrievably broken? A soul who needs to know Him? Is He holding out a world to delight in? An opportunity to learn more about Him and become more like Him?

Can you take what He offers? Are you willing to see that He is here and He is good and He also wants to pull you out of the clutter and toward that "immeasurably more"?

Such unremitting love can make us uncomfortable, because we don't feel we deserve it. We've been disappointed so often—will God pull the rug out from under us? Might He ask something of us that we don't feel equipped to do?

Niagara is scary. It's not safe or intimate; just as we can't look upon the face of the Living God, we can't jump off the precipice. The trickle from a hose is a lot more familiar.

But there's something incredibly exhilarating . . . something *large* . . . about standing on its brink. Go ahead—jump! Because God's hands will be there to hold you up.

Notes

1. New York: HarperCollins Children's Books.

14
Imagine a Gift . . .

AND FINALLY—think about the greatest thing that could happen to you.

Imagine being given, out of the blue, something you had always wanted but never dreamed you could attain. Imagine, for example, waking up and finding yourself twenty pounds thinner. Think about how you would feel if an anonymous benefactor paid for college for your children, if you and your husband were somehow enabled to quit your jobs and go on the mission field as you've always dreamed, if some chronic illness in your family was cured.

Then put yourself in Peter's sandals.

You're a fisherman, like your father before you. Early in the morning, you're washing your nets. You're weary and sore; all night you've been out on the lake trying to catch fish, but either the lake is fished out or they've all gone to the other end. You've come up empty. And this is your livelihood: no fish, no money.

Then this Nazarene you've dimly heard about asks you to row him out a little ways from shore. Well, all right; the work is done for the day, and the water helps voices carry. So you push out and half listen.

But *then* he turns to you and says something startling. (You don't know this, but this is the first of many startling things you will hear from this Nazarene.) "Put out into deep water, and let down the nets for a catch."

Obviously not a fisherman! You protest, but something in his look and voice moves you to do as he says. You row farther out, to around the same spot where you fished in vain under the stars last night. You let down the nets.

And then . . .

The boat lurches and jerks. What is this? You grab for the nets—and they are so full of fish you can't handle them all. You shout and wave for James and John to come help.

Who is this man who fills your boats?

All your life, since you were old enough to handle an oar, this has been the greatest thing that could happen to you, all these fish! A dream come true! But you do not think about this. You forget your catch, all these fish that weigh down your boat, and turn instead to the Nazarene, flinging yourself at his feet. "Lord! I do not deserve this! I do not deserve you!" Your life up until now has been straightforward, the sea and the fish and the synagogue; but you sense, with a strange mixture of fear and awe and hope, that it is about to take a huge turn.

With *him*.

And you go.

What this account out of Luke 5 tells me is this: As great as the gifts God gives us, there is something greater—himself. Peter, the rough fisherman, understood this. His first response could have been an exultant, "Let's take this catch to market!" He could have thanked Jesus, praised God for the miracle, and then returned to his work. He didn't. He fell before the Master, seeing only Him.

But there's more. Now, think about those times of loneliness and discouragement, times you've felt abandoned, times when you've seriously questioned, *Is all this real?*

Where are you, God? And put yourself in Peter's place again. . . .

It is night. You are hanging around a chilly courtyard, hoping not to be noticed by the servants who gather around a fire to keep warm. But you are seen: "There's one who was with the Nazarene!"

As great as the gifts God gives us are, there is something greater—himself.

What do you say? If you say yes, will they take you away, too? You shake your head. "I don't know him!"

"Listen to his accent! This man is a Galilean!"

"I tell you, I am not!" you shout, twice more. And you run away weeping.

The Master predicted this. He knew the frailties of men. Of you. He was the most wonderful thing that ever happened to you, and now, as you are about to lose Him, you have turned away.

Days later you and the others are in the hiding place, wondering what to do next, when there is a knock. You open the door to two women. What could they want at this hour? Are you and the others in danger, too?

And then you find out, and you go running to see for yourself, hoping against hope. . . .

I see myself in both these stories. There are times when I want only Jesus, when I would follow Him anywhere. And then there are times when I backslide, when my resounding "Yes!" shrinks into a timid "I'm not sure," when my behavior declares, "I don't know the man!"

But Jesus never turns away. He comes and says, "Woman, why do you weep? Why do you turn away? Touch my hand. I'm real. Come and have breakfast—I know you like fish. Sit with me awhile. Because I'm not going anywhere. I will never, never leave you."

We call out, "I know you're here, Lord . . . somewhere." And He responds, "Here I am! And here! And here!" Working in us. Pulling us. Guiding us. Inviting us. Changing us. But in the end, beyond what He does with and for us, He is all there is.

Here He comes now, bearing the Living Water. Let's hold our breath, leap in, and splash around!

Books to Help You Along the Way

HERE'S AN ARBITRARY and necessarily incomplete list of places I've found help on my spiritual journey and in puzzling out my life in general. I'd like you to know about them. Some of your favorites may be missing, but maybe I don't know about them. Write me in care of this publisher and let me know what they are! I hope it helps.

- **Scripture.** I prefer the New International Version for its clarity without sacrificing a certain majesty and force to the language. The *Quest Study Bible*, copublished by Zondervan and Christianity Today, Inc., is a very helpful new (1994) addition to study Bibles. It includes answers to questions real people have asked about themes, events, and characters in Scripture, in a readable and accessible format. Eugene Peterson's paraphrase of the New Testament, *The Message* (NavPress), is fine for devotional reading.
- **Prayer.** I have found Ole Hallesby's slim classic *Prayer* (I use the Augsburg paperback) to be filled with wisdom and insight. Hallesby was a Norwegian seminary professor. Though the book was published in 1931, the problems he

addresses are timeless. When I read this book I have the feeling of sitting at the feet of a godly and learned man who nevertheless is taking time to explain things to me in simple, direct language.

■ **Life Questions.** *Between Two Truths: Living With Biblical Tensions*, by New Testament scholar Klyne Snodgrass (Zondervan), addresses seeming paradoxes in Scripture—law and grace, faith and works—and applies them to life in the manner of a finely exegeted sermon. Snodgrass went directly to the original Greek texts for his sources and communicates his ideas with a strong and refreshingly realistic sense of what everyday Christians struggle with. This short paperback would be an excellent book for a fairly advanced study group.

Wrestling With Angels, a video series produced by Trinity Church in New York City and Zondervan Video, looks at issues such as guidance, doubt, suffering, prayer, forgiveness, and how to love oneself and others. The series combines the wisdom of well-known communicators (Tony Campolo on guidance, Lewis Smedes on forgiveness) with reflections from real people—and, often, the comments from the real folk are even more insightful than those of the experts. The eight-week format is ideal for a church quarter. Comes with a study guide.

■ **Spiritual Disciplines.** Dallas Willard's *The Spirit of the Disciplines* (Harper San Francisco) is not always easy going, but worth exploring for its emphasis on what it means to actually follow Jesus, and how to engage in practices—from celebration to frugality—that will help the believer become more Christlike.

■ **Seeking God.** In all his writing and speaking, Christian psychologist Larry Crabb has always impressed me with his passion for honesty, for digging below the surface of things. In his book *Finding God* (Zondervan), he reveals his struggles to know God—his doubts, his questions, his ultimate surrender. While I think Crabb overstates his thesis (that is, people are more concerned with their problems than finding God) and is too quick to dismiss readers' needs for hope and help, this book offers a moving story of one man's search.

Anything by *John Fischer*. He's written three collections of essays and two novels, all published by Bethany House Publishers, and the theme of his work is constant and provocative, challenging evangelicals to peel away layers of unexamined thinking and get to the truth about God and His church. There are times when Fischer seems to dwell on critique at the expense of constructive vision, but he makes a very entertaining iconoclast.

- **Devotional Aids.** There's a raft of fine material, of course; but I especially appreciate Bethany House Publishers' series REKINDLING THE INNER FIRE, slim paperbacks that introduce readers to the works of such spiritual masters as Augustine and Amy Carmichael. "Classic" Christian writers can be difficult reading, but series editor David Hazard has made them accessible without dumbing down the ideas. Highly recommended.

- **The Church.** Charles Colson just seems to keep coming out with these substantial, prophetic books that speak to our condition at the end of the century. One of the most significant is *The Body* (Word), written with Ellen Santilli Vaughn, a powerful call for evangelicals to rediscover the importance of the church. Colson's and Vaughn's stories of the persecuted, yet persevering, church in Eastern Europe are gripping and inspiring. This, too, would be a fine book for a group study.

- **Self-discovery.** For those interested in more intentionally pursuing who they are and what God may have for them, *A Life You Can Love*, by Diane Eble (Zondervan), offers very helpful guidance. It's also a good introduction to the "type theory" of personalities.

This and That. . . Reality and the Vision (Word) is a collection of well-known Christian writers discussing writers *they* admire—for example, Walter Wangerin, Jr., on Hans Christian Andersen, Karen Burton Mains on

Aleksandr Solzhenitsyn, John Leax on Thomas Merton. I include it in this list because it's more than just a book for literary types—it tells stories that shed new light on God.

How to Eat Humble Pie & Not Get Indigestion, by Charlene Ann Baumbich (InterVarsity), tells stories too—hilarious, often profound stories of a woman's search for humility. The author has a gift for the anecdote that can push us toward a greater understanding of God, but she also uses Scripture effectively. I saw myself many times in this book, and I squirmed—and then I was encouraged.

Laugh Again, by Charles R. Swindoll (Word). It always amazes me how *irrepressible* Swindoll is. Some preachers think that a canned story equals humor. Not Chuck Swindoll. He's an original all the way. I know of no other communicator who combines storytelling, solid scriptural interpretation, and the sense of listening to a real person as well as he does. This study of Philippians reminds us of how joyful Paul could be, and how Christians should be.

Everything in the world by *C. S. Lewis*. I find myself returning to both his fiction and nonfiction over and over. He enlarges my view of God, he challenges and reassures me, and every now and then he'll slip in some devastating bit of wit. Most of all, he gives his readers the gift of *himself* through his writings. It's like having a friend who's wise and generous and funny and imaginative—a friend who points you toward God.

Acknowledgments

AS ALWAYS, I couldn't have written this book without David Hazard, one of the wisest and most creative editors in Christendom. Helen Motter's fine hand shaped and sharpened the material and made it better. I appreciate the encouragement and support of Bethany House's Kevin Johnson, as well as Gary and Carol Johnson, whose leadership and example help put the "Christian" back into "Christian publishing."

I'm really, really thankful for Diane Eble, Eileen Silva Kindig, and Barb Tennyson, as well as the "kitchen group" at Faith Church. I also want to give due credit to a number of people—Jack Armbruster, Cheri Auman, Jeff Crafton, Sue Aarseth, O'Ann Steere—whose ideas and insights made me go, "Aha! They're on to something!" I'm eternally grateful for Jan Gustafson, whom I firmly believe is God-sent; and for all the pastors whose preaching and teaching I've been privileged to sit under—John Benson, Greg Mesimore, Dave Philips, Chris Lyons, Charles Austin, and many more. My husband, Fritz, and daughter, Amanda, remain, as always, the lights of my life.

To God be the glory.